Past-into-Present Series

ELECTIONS

Peter Lane

Principal Lecturer in History,
Coloma College of Education

B. T. BATSFORD LTD London

First published 1973
© Peter Lane 1973

Printed in Great Britain by
Redwood Press Limited, Trowbridge, Wiltshire
for the publishers
B. T. Batsford Ltd, 4 Fitzhardinge Street, London, W1H 0AH

ISBN 0 7134 1781 1

Acknowledgment

The Author and Publisher wish to thank the following for the illustrations which appear in this book: Camera Press for figs 4, 47; the *Daily Express* for fig 55; the *Daily Mail* for fig 52; *Glasgow Herald* for fig 53; Keystone Press for figs 49, 61, 62, 63, 64; London Transport for fig 48; the Mansell Collection for figs 2, 3, 13, 14, 15, 16, 19, 22, 25, 28 29, 30, 31, 32, 35, 37, 38, 39; the National Portrait Gallery for fig 5; *The New Statesman* for fig 60; *The Observer* for fig 57; Popperphotos for fig 54; the Press Association for figs 1, 56; Radio Times Hulton Picture Library for figs 20, 27, 33, 34, 41, 43, 44, 45 46, 50, 51, 59; *The Spectator* for fig 58.

Fig 34 is Crown copyright and is reproduced by permission of the Controller of HM Stationery Office.

They also wish to thank Macmillan, London and Basingstoke, for permission to quote extracts from *The British General Election* by Butler and King, and from *Wind of Change* by Harold Macmillan; and the Hamlyn Publishing Group Ltd for extracts from *Herbert Morrison, An Autobiography*.

Contents

The Illustrations

Introduction

Every year the main political parties hold a conference, and if you listen to the speeches of the leaders or read the reports in the newspapers it will be evident that hardly is one general election over than we are all looking towards the next, despite the fact that it will probably not be held for nearly four years. The researchers of the opinion polls will be at work assessing the trends of public opinion and the popularity of the parties. It seems that the country lives in a state of permanent election fever. If this is so, then we who are the victims of this disease ought to have some idea of its nature.

The electoral system

Today almost everyone over the age of eighteen is entitled to vote at an election and only members of the House of Lords, prisoners and lunatics do not have the *franchise* (or the right to vote). The country is divided into *constituencies* in which live about 75,000 voters; because of rebuilding and redevelopment the number of voters living in various constituencies is continually changing, so Parliament has set up a Boundaries Commission to examine these changes and to recommend changes in the areas covered by constituencies.

This system is very modern. In 1784 (Chapter 1) and 1831 (Chapter 2) there were three types of constituency—the *Universities* of Oxford and Cambridge returned their own MPs, elected by graduates of those Universities. Each *County*, regardless of size, returned two MPs so that the 15,000 Yorkshire voters had the same value as the 600 Rutland voters. Then there were the *Boroughs*. These varied in type: some were known as *pot-walloper* boroughs, because the vote was given to every householder who could show that he had a fireplace capable of boiling a pot; others were *scot-and-lot* boroughs where every ratepayer was allowed

Trafalgar Square on the night of the general election 1970. The crowd are watching the results being flashed onto the gigantic screen

to vote. There were *freemen* boroughs where only the few people who had been awarded the freedom of the borough could vote, and *corporation* boroughs where only the members of the town council could vote. A large number were *rotten* boroughs, where only a small number of people had the vote.

Unlike our modern system, which is uniform, in those days people could change their political rights by moving to another area. If a 'pot-walloper' left his borough to live in a 'freemen' borough he also lost the right to vote while, on the other hand, a non-voter in a 'corporation' borough could gain a vote if he moved to a 'scot-and-lot' borough and became a ratepayer. There were even one or two places such as Westminster which allowed every man who had spent the previous night in the borough to have a vote (Chapter 1).

Former voters

In the county elections every man who owned the freehold of land worth forty shillings (£2) a year had the right to vote. This at least was a uniform practice throughout the whole country, and meant that the voter was less likely to be open to a landowner's persuasion than if he were merely a tenant. However, it did mean that very wealthy (and possibly very independent-minded) men who only rented farms and estates did not have the right to vote—although their estates might have been much larger than that of a forty shilling freeholder.

First Reform Act, 1832

The Reform Act, 1832, established a simple and universal qualification for the franchise. In the county constituencies the forty shilling freeholder was joined by better-off tenant farmers—those who had long leases of land rated at £10 a year, those who had short leases of land rated at £50 a year and tenants who paid a rent of £50 a year. In the boroughs the Act abolished all the old, variable franchises and the right to vote was given to any man who owned or rented a property which had been valued by the rating officer as worth £10 a year. We have to remember that money values have changed. In 1832 the Metropolitan Police Force paid its constables 12s 6d (62½p) per week. Today, the same constables are paid over £25 a week. Taking this as an indication, we have to multiply 1832 figures by at least 40 to get a modern equivalent; this means that the vote was given to people who owned or rented houses rated at the modern equivalent of £400 a year. These were very rich men indeed, and it is not surprising that even after this Reform Act only about 650,000 men were allowed to vote.

The 1832 Act also affected the constituencies. Fifty-six boroughs with populations of under 2,000 lost their right to have MPs, while thirty others were deprived of one seat but allowed to retain one. The seats available were then distributed

This Act recognised the growing importance of the rich industrial middle class, some of whom could now vote, and also the existence of some of the new industrial towns and cities, some of which were now to be represented in Parliament for the first time.

2 A woman recording her vote in the first election after the 1918 Reform Act which gave the vote to women over 30. The box in which she is placing her vote will be collected and the votes counted when the polling station closes

Second Reform Act, 1867

The 1867 Reform Act was a much more sweeping one than that of 1832—which deserves credit, however, as being a step along the road to democracy. The 1867 Act gave the franchise in the boroughs to every adult male occupier of a house; in general the people who gained the vote under this reform were the skilled working classes who by 1867 had strong trade unions, good wages and standards of living that their parents could never have hoped for. The Act also altered the constituency arrangements:

38 boroughs were in future to return only one member;

the City of Manchester and the Boroughs of Liverpool, Birmingham and Leeds would each respectively return three members;

ten new boroughs were created, and others reorganised;

thirteen new county divisions were created;

the University of London was to return one member.

7

3 *Voting in 1910*, a painting by S. Begg. The supervising clerks (on the right) have to ensure that no-one tries to vote twice or to impersonate some other voter. The voter has marked his ballot paper in the secrecy of the booth (on the left) and is now putting his paper in the ballot box. The police sergeant is on duty to ensure that there is no trouble

Electoral laws, 1872 and 1883

The 1874 election was the first general election in which the ballot box was used. Up until 1872, when the Ballot Act was passed, elections were held at the *hustings*—a temporary stand put up in the main street or square. Here the Returning Officer sat with his Polling Book which showed the names of all those who were entitled to vote. Each page of the book was ruled off in columns from top to bottom, the names of the various candidates standing at the top of different columns. When a voter was ready he climbed the ladder to the platform on which the Returning Officer sat with the candidates and their friends. After proving that he had the right to vote—by giving his name and address—the voter then announced in public the name of the candidate for whom he wished to vote. Down below, the candidates' agents had assembled crowds of supporters—few, if any, of whom had the right to vote; most of them were paid to come along and stand with the brass band which was paid for by the candidate. When the mob heard the voter's intentions they broke out into cheering (if their candidate had got another vote) or into booing. When the voter came down the stairs he was surrounded by the rival gangs—one eager to carry him off to the nearest alehouse, the other eager to throw him in the river. More significantly, the candidates' agents had heard which way he had cast his vote—and could arrange for him to be rewarded or punished as the case may be. If he had supported the government candidate then the reward might be a job in the civil service for one of his relatives, a contract for materials required by the army or navy or just a straightforward money bribe. Where there was a very important employer supporting a particular candidate, a vote against that candidate could mean the loss of a job or eviction from a house.

The Ballot Act, 1872, was meant to end this. After 1872 no-one would know in which way a person had voted and so no-one could be punished or rewarded. The Corrupt Practices Act, 1883, set limits to the amount a candidate could spend on an election, so that thereafter a rich candidate would not be able to get extra support by straightforward bribery, or by such practices as hiring all the cabs, paying double the price asked for in hotels and alehouses and so on.

The Third Reform Act, 1884 and the Redistribution of Seats Act, 1885

The 1884 Act extended the terms of the 1867 Act to the county voter so that all male adult householders throughout the country could now vote. This was a very big step along the road to at least a male democracy—although about half the men in the country still did not have the vote since they were not householders —perhaps they were sons living at home, lodgers paying a low rent, occupiers of one or two rooms in slum housing.

The 1885 Act was also important because it changed the constituency pattern very significantly to give fairer representation.

Democracy, 1918–1928

In 1918 Parliament passed an Act which extended the franchise to all men over the age of twenty-one and all women over the age of thirty; this ridiculous differentiation between men and women was abolished by an Act of 1928 which gave the vote to all women over the age of twenty-one. At last Britain had come to the end of the road along which she had taken the first steps in 1832. By 1928 Britain was an adult democracy in which almost everyone over the age of twenty-one could vote, in secret, and without being unduly influenced by a wealthy candidate.

However, it was not quite the end of the road because in 1969 the franchise was extended to people over the age of eighteen. We have seen that the right to vote had previously been connected with the ownership or occupation of property —a person had to be a freeholder, or a tenant, or a ratepayer, or have some connection with property in order to qualify for a vote. Since the law had fixed twenty-one as the age at which people could legally own property, enter into financial agreements (such as hire purchase), it seemed logical for Parliament to fix the democratic voting age at twenty-one. However, once the government had changed the law on property and debts, it was logical to change the law on the voting age.

What differences have been produced by this mass participation in elections? How different are modern elections from those of the early nineteenth century

(Chapter 2) when, in some constituencies, only one or two people, and in others no-one at all, voted? How has this change affected the policies proposed by the opposing politicians? Do modern politicians make the same kind of promises as did politicians in, say, 1784 (Chapter 1), when the government of the country was the concern mainly of the upper class?

Prime Ministers

When the election is over, the leader of the Party with the largest number of seats, is invited by the Monarch to form a government. Like so much of the electoral process this is a modern development. In the seventeenth century the Monarch was his own Prime Minister, sitting with his Council which he chose as he wished without reference to Parliament. In the eighteenth century the Monarch's power was limited by the 1688 Revolution and the Acts which followed it; the King had the right to choose whoever he wanted as his Chief Minister, but his chosen one had to be able to gain a majority vote in the Commons. This remained the situation until the nineteenth century when Queen Victoria tried, unsuccessfully, to stop Peel from becoming Prime Minister, and showed that she did not want Gladstone to be Prime Minister of a Liberal government in 1880. By this time the Monarch's power had been further limited; in a more democratic age the politicians claimed the right to choose their own leaders.

In the modern Labour Party the Party leader is elected, each autumn, by the Parliamentary Labour Party. If a Labour Prime Minister were to die while in office, the Monarch would wait until the Party had chosen a successor before inviting anyone to form a new government. The Monarch's power is very limited in this case. Until very recently the situation was different in the Conservative Party, which did not elect its leader as the Labour Party does. When a Conservative Prime Minister died or retired, the Monarch—in theory at any rate—was free to choose anyone as the next Prime Minister without reference to the Party. In fact, of course, the Monarch always asked for advice. In 1922 Bonar Law, then Prime Minister, was forced to retire owing to ill-health. King George V, through his Private Secretary, took the advice of leading Conservatives—notably a former Conservative Prime Minister, Balfour, and then invited Stanley Baldwin to become Prime Minister, although many outside observers believed that Lord Curzon would be chosen. In 1940 when Parliamentary pressure forced Neville Chamberlain to resign, King George VI took advice from Conservative and Labour leaders before asking Winston Churchill, rather than Lord Halifax, to become Prime Minister. Churchill's first action was to call a meeting of the Conservative Party and get himself appointed Party leader. In more modern times the resignation of Sir Anthony Eden and the later resignation of Harold Macmillan led to a great deal of publicity surrounding the almost mysterious process by which the Party chose its leaders. As a result of the unfortunate publicity surrounding these events, the Party decided to follow Labour's lead

4 Counting the votes. On the left a clerk is counting the votes cast for a candidate; on the right another box is being emptied and clerks are waiting to put the ballot papers into piles according to the ways in which people have voted. The standing onlookers are representatives of the various political parties who watch the count to ensure that no mistakes are made by the hurrying clerks

In 1965, when Sir Alec Douglas Home resigned as Party Leader, the Conservatives asked Conservative MPs, Conservative members of the House of Lords and prospective Conservative candidates to meet and elect their leader. Reginald Maudling and Enoch Powell were the unsuccessful candidates in the election, in which the Conservatives chose Edward Heath as their leader. In future, the Monarch's power will be limited to inviting whoever is chosen to become Prime Minister.

Election day

In the eighteenth century the general elections were carried on over forty days, but since 1918 the election must take place on one day. Throughout the country, polling booths are opened at the same time on that particular election day; they close at the same time in the night. In every constituency, registration officers supervise the counting of votes and within twenty-four hours of the closing of the polling booths the result of the election has been announced in nearly every constituency.

What difference has this change made to the business of canvassing? Why was bribery more likely in a long-drawn-out election than in our modern, one-day affair?

Social change

Some elections are more important than others. If, for example, a Tory government has ruled for nearly forty years and is then replaced by a Whig government (Chapter 2) we should expect some change in the direction of government legislation. When the Labour Party first won a majority in the House of Commons (Chapter 8), the country entered upon the 'greatest social revolution in our history' according to Sir Robert Boothby, speaking at a Conservative Party Conference in 1949. Some elections do not produce this sort of great change; when, for example, the Labour Party won the election of 1950 the new government merely carried on with the policies of the previous government; the Prime Minister before the election merely returned to Number 10 Downing Street as Prime Minister again. Which elections have produced the greatest degree of change? Was the election of 1830 more important than, say, the election of 1852?

In this book we will examine the story of ten elections and try to find out the answers to some of the questions. Of course there were other elections which we might have chosen to illustrate the answers. The chosen examples are not intended to be exhaustive but only illustrative.

1 1784: A Schoolboy Prime Minister and a Forty-day Election

Parliament, 1784

On 25 March 1784, George III dismissed the Parliament which had been elected in 1780 and which had expected to sit until 1787, when the next general election was due. The King acted in what was then an unusual way on the advice of his twenty-four year old Prime Minister, William Pitt the Younger. Members of Parliament left the House of Commons, which had been described in 1782 by C. P. Morritz:

> Members of the House of Commons have nothing particular in their dress, they even come into the House in their great coats, and with boots and spurs. It is not at all uncommon to see a member lying stretched out on one of the benches, while others are debating. Some crack nuts, others eat oranges or whatever else is in season. . . . Those who speak deliver themselves with little

5 The House of Commons in 1833

gravity. All that is necessary is to stand up in your place, take off your hat and stick in one hand, and with the other hand to make any such motions as you fancy necessary.

The first day that I was at the House of Commons, the debate happened to be whether besides being made a peer, any other specific reward should be bestowed by the nation on their gallant admiral Rodney. In the course of the debate, I remember, Fox was very sharply reprimanded by young Lord Fielding for having opposed the election of Admiral Hood as a member for Westminster. Fox was sitting not far from the table on which the gilt sceptre lay. He now took his place so near it that he could reach it with his hand, and thus placed he gave it many a hearty thump. . . . It is impossible for me to describe with what fire and persuasive eloquence he spoke, and how the Speaker in the chair incessantly nodded approbation from beneath his solemn wig; and innumerable voices incessantly called out 'Hear him! Hear him!' and when there was the least sign that he intended to leave off speaking, they no less vociferously exclaimed 'Go on!'; and so he continued to speak in this manner for nearly two hours.

Elections—many styles

All the MPs were anxious to be returned once again, because they agreed with Admiral Lord Rodney that 'to be out of Parliament is to be out of the world'. Those who represented one of the 'rotten' constituencies had only to make an agreement with the owner of the constituency to be assured of their return to Parliament. Sir Francis Burdett bought his seat at Boroughbridge from the Duke of Newcastle, signing the agreement which read: 'That it is agreed between the Trustees of the . . . Duke of Newcastle and Mr Thomas Coutts—that on Francis Burdett Esq being returned a member to serve in the ensuing Parliament . . . Mr Coutts shall pay the sum of Four Thousand Pounds towards discharging the Debt due to him by the Duke . . . if Parliament shall be dissolved before having sat for . . . six years, The Trustees promise . . . to bring the said Mr Burdett in again to Parliament to sit for such time as . . . shall complete the period of six years in all, and no longer. At the end of which period Mr Coutts undertakes that Mr Burdett shall pledge his honour to vacate his seat.'

Others had to contest an election with an opponent equally anxious to get into Parliament. Such an election might cost each candidate up to £30,000. Some candidates tried to limit the expense involved by making an agreement with their opponents, as happened in Northampton where there were about 1,000 voters. The three Earls contesting this seat agreed:

1 That mobbings of all kinds shall be discontinued . . . until the election shall be over.

2 That no house be opened at any time or any ticket given for drink or liquor by the above-mentioned . . . until the day of election, except on seven days notice to the gentlemen who sign this paper.

14

3 That if on any occasion houses should be opened after seven days notice, it shall be done by tickets for drink given to the men inhabitants, half-a-crown to drink to those who have promised one vote and a crown to drink to those who have promised two...

4 That the damage done to the windows of the George Inn be repaired at a joint expense.

Most constituencies were not contested at all; the potential candidates took a quick canvass of the electorate and if they discovered that minds had already been made up, the probable loser withdrew—to save himself needless expense.

The Westminster election, 1784

Westminster was one of the few more democratic constituencies since the vote was given to every adult male sleeping in the constituency on the night of the opening of the election. Here, in 1784, Admiral Lord Hood and Sir Cecil Wray stood as candidates supporting Pitt's government, while Charles James Fox, a former Foreign Secretary, stood as the leading opponent to 'this schoolboy's government'. There was no doubt that Hood, the gallant Admiral, would be elected; the real interest was in the contest for the second seat. Would Wray or Fox win this? Would Pitt's supporter defeat his enemy?

6 The famous Duchess of Devonshire, who supported Fox by offering to kiss all those who promised to vote for her favourite in the Westminster election, 1784

From 1 April 1784, until the poll closed on 17 May 1784, the electorate enjoyed the sight of the most famous canvassing campaign in history. Duchesses, siding with one side and the other, offered 'their favours' to the electorate in return for a promise to vote in a particular way. Under the open system of voting a man had to declare publicly to the returning officer; his decision was openly known and few would have dared to accept the favours of the beautiful Duchess of Devonshire and then cast his vote against her candidate, Fox. Elections are less interesting today now that this sort of canvassing has been made illegal.

Charles James Fox

Charles James Fox had been the leading opponent of the government led by Lord North (1770–1782) and of its policy which drove the Americans to rebel. Fox had described George III as a potential Charles I, trying to re-establish the power of the monarchy. In 1780, George III had used the vast influence of the Crown to bribe enough constituencies to return MPs who would support North's government, but Fox had managed to win the support of some constituencies where there were more democratic elections. He was able to present to Parliament a series of 'addresses' from various boroughs, demanding reforms of Parliament—including annual elections—an end to the American War, a change in government policy, and the dismissal of Lord North. However, Lord North continued in office: the government had been elected in 1780 and was not to be put off by a series of addresses; government would be almost impossible if it had to change its policies to fit in with every opinion poll. After 1780, North became increasingly popular with the very people who had once signed the hostile 'addresses'. This was because the war against the Americans was widened into a war against Holland, France and Spain as these countries, hoping to take advantage of Britain's difficulties, declared war and tried to cripple Britain's trade.

On 20 March 1782 North fell from power and was replaced by the Whig, Rockingham, who appointed Fox as Foreign Secretary. To oppose the government in these circumstances could easily be seen as an act of treachery; Fox was suspected of being a pro-French opponent of British power, trade and influence. When Lord Rodney won the notable battle of the Saints (May 1782) in the West Indies, the country rejoiced; Fox, now Foreign Secretary, recalled the victorious Admiral and replaced him by a less capable admiral, Pigot. The popular opinion was that Fox did not want Britain to take advantage of this victory.

The aged Rockingham died in July 1782 and was replaced by another Whig, Shelburne, who dismissed Fox and invited Pitt into his Cabinet as Chancellor of the Exchequer. The Shelburne government continued to try to make peace with America—which naturally annoyed the followers of Lord North who had led the country during the War. Fox, the former opponent of the War (and of North), now joined forces with North to oppose the Peace and to force the Commons to vote for the dismissal of Shelburne. In March 1783 the King was forced to invite North and Fox to form a Ministry.

7 *Britannia's Assassination* by Gillray. An American Indian is running off with the head, pursued by an empty-handed France; Spain has got a leg and Holland has taken the shield. While Judges Thurlow and Mansfield try to protect Britannia, Fox is biting her leg and Wilkes is hitting out with his magazine, *North Briton*

Fox in power

In November 1783 Fox introduced his India Bill by which the government meant to take power from the East India Company and transfer it to the government. Some sort of reform was needed in the case of the East India Company, which had started off as a trading company but had conquered huge portions of Indian territory so that the company now ruled over Bengal, the Carnatic, Bombay and other parts of India. Merchants whose lives had been spent in trading were not trained to rule, and serious mistakes had been made in India, so reform was needed; but Fox's proposals were seen as an outrageous attempt to transfer the power of the Company to himself and his friends. This was contrary to the spirit of the 1688 Revolution, by which the policy of the government was supposed to be the policy of the Monarch.

The King had never liked Fox—his long-time opponent—and he was anxious to get rid of this Ministry. He could not persuade enough MPs to vote against the India Bill in November 1783, but when the Bill went to the House of Lords George III used his influence with the Lords, who threw the Bill out on

8 *(left) Carlo Khan's Triumphant Entry into Leadenhall Street*, by Sayers. Fox, dressed as an oriental prince, is riding an elephant with the face of Lord North, while Burke is leading the animal towards India House

9 *(below) The Hanoverian Horse and the British Lion* by Rowlandson. Pitt is riding the horse (the King) which is kicking at Fox, who is riding the British Lion. The horse is trampling on 'Magna Carta', 'Bill of Rights' and 'Constitution'. The lion fears that the horse will become too powerful while the horse claims that it is exercising only the prerogative (or right) of the King to dissolve Parliament

17 December. The King immediately dismissed Fox and North, and appointed Pitt as his Chief Minister.

William Pitt

William Pitt the Younger, son of the famous William Pitt, was born in 1759, his father's 'miracle year' when, under his leadership, Britain won several outstanding victories over France and won Canada, India and several islands in the West Indies. The younger Pitt had entered Parliament as a follower of Shelburne, a Whig who hoped to lead a Ministry containing men of all political parties. Pitt had refused a post in Rockingham's government, but under Shelburne, Pitt had been Chancellor of the Exchequer when only 23—the youngest Cabinet Minister of all time. George III appointed him to lead the government when he was only 24 and the youngest Prime Minister of all time. In December 1783 Pitt took office, to be mocked by Fox as a 'schoolboy' leading a 'mincepie administration' which would be dismissed once the mincepies of Christmas, 1783 had been eaten.

Prime Minister Pitt

At first Young Pitt faced a hostile Commons; many MPs may have opposed the Fox-North India Bill but they disliked the King using his influence to persuade the Lords to throw that government out of office. Pitt's courage, honesty and

10 *The Mirror of Patriotism* by Sayers. Fox is looking in the mirror as he rehearses a speech, but his reflection is that of Oliver Cromwell. Fox's opposition to George III laid him open to the accusation that he wanted to be another dictator

determination soon persuaded many MPs that here was a great leader, not some-one easily controlled by the King nor someone out for his own gain—as Fox had obviously been in 1783. John Robinson, a former Treasury secretary, helped Pitt, through the government, to win the support of the many independent MPs in the House. This could be done by offering a job, a contract or a title to an MP, who promised to support the government. It had been done before as Edward Gibbon found out in 1779: 'By . . . the favourable disposition of Lord North, I was appointed one of the Lords Commissioners of Trade and Plantations (1779); and my private income was enlarged by a clear addition of between seven and eight hundred pounds a year . . . it must be allowed that our duty was not in-tolerably severe, and that I enjoyed many days and weeks of repose, without being called away from my library to the office'. In Walpole's phrase, 'every man has his price'.

The MPs who changed sides and began to support Pitt were known as 'Robinson's Rats' by Fox, whose support dwindled. Throughout the country Pitt became more popular. When he thought that he had won a sufficient following—in March 1784—he asked the King to dismiss Parliament and call for an election. Fox and his followers argued that the King had no right to do this; Parliament had been elected in 1780 and should sit until 1787; the government was not popular in the country—and Fox waved the 'loyal addresses' signed by his supporters as proof that the country wanted a change of government. By now many people had shown in cartoons, songs, poems and newspaper articles, that Fox was a self-seeking politician, comparable perhaps to Cromwell in his desire to limit the power of the King, not caring which argument he used so long as he advanced his own interest. In 1782 he had argued that the Parliament had been corruptly elected and the country needed a new election to get rid of North; now he was arguing that this same Parliament—in which he had a large following—was properly elected and should be allowed to choose its own Ministers.

On 14 February 1784, at a meeting of his own Westminster electors, Fox was shouted down with cries of 'No grand mogul; no India tyrant; no turncoat'—cries indicating that he was no longer the darling of the crowd. The electorate understood that the real issue in the election was whether the King had to accept Ministers and policies against his will. Pitt appreciated this position. In 1801 he wanted to pass the Catholic Emancipation Act; when George III indicated that he could not approve such an Act, Pitt resigned his office.

For the first twenty days of the election Fox seemed certain to lose; but by the twenty-third day he had more votes than Wray, his rival. Admiral Hood called on sailors to make mobs to shout in support of Wray and insults about Fox. Fox invited the Irish to create another rival mob to act on his behalf. There were songs, poems, cartoons, posters, newspaper articles, all helping to create a great degree of excitement in the constituency. Above all, there was the Duchess of Devonshire, Fox's main supporter and active canvasser. When she left London in the middle of the election to look after her sick mother, she was recalled by the

Duchess of Portland, who wrote on 13 April: 'I am almost worn out; if we should lose it is owing to your absence'. The Duchess herself wrote to her mother: 'I am unhappy here beyond measure and abused for nothing. Yet as it is begun I must go on with it. My sister and another Lady were both kissed, so it's very hard that I, who was not, should have the reputation for it.' One of the posters put out by Hood and Wray read: 'To be hired for the day, several pairs of ruby, pouting lips of the first quality'. Fox also had the support of other fashionable beauties—Mrs Crewe, Lady Duncannon and both Ladies Waldegrave. On the other hand, Wray was supported by Lady Salisbury and a Mrs Hobart who, aged 45, and very fat, was not a serious rival to the beauties on Fox's side. All these ladies carried the voters to the poll in their own coaches—a useful aid to the candidate in a widespread constituency and particularly valuable as a bribe to the poorer voters.

The result

The election only ended because polling could not last more than forty days. Fox beat Wray by 246 votes, the figures being:

Hood	6,694
Fox	6,234
Wray	5,988

Elsewhere Fox's supporters lost heavily to their Pittite opponents; the youthful, honest and courageous Pitt had won that support which he needed and in the process had driven many former MPs out into the wilderness. These 'Fox's martyrs' must have taken small comfort from the success of Fox himself who was able to say:

> Our Westminster, Norwich and London successes
> Are a glorious comment on your boasted addresses

Even these boasted 'successes' were poor ones; in every constituency the Pittite candidate gained the first seat and the Foxite had to be content with the second.

11 *The Poll* by Rowlandson. Mrs Hobart (the supporter of Pitt's candidate, Wray) is held down by Admiral Hood and outweighs the Duchess of Devonshire whom Fox is trying to help. The bare bosoms and the watching crowd give some indication of the nature of elections in the eighteenth century

The long-term result

The election over, the temperature dropped and life in Westminster returned to some sort of normality; the Duchesses returned to their lives of leisure and the voters to their work-a-day world. But for Pitt the election was the beginning of a great Ministry which, with a slight interruption, lasted until his death in 1806. During this time the French Revolution disrupted the peace of Europe, and Pitt led England into a series of Coalitions and Wars against France and Napoleon. Fox, on the other hand, became the supporter and defender of the French and the opponent of the British attempt to undo the French Revolution. In this period a new Tory Party was born; its leader Pitt, the former Whig; its policies to uphold the power of Britain. Fox led a small Whig Party with its principles of freedom, religious and political toleration. And there was never again a dispute as to whether the King, advised by the Prime Minister, had the right to dissolve Parliament and call an election. Today that is one of the Prime Minister's most important powers—a power which Fox, the Liberal, would have denied him.

2　1831: The Great Reform Bill Election

1830–1831 Years of revolution

Many general elections have created a spirit of excitement and unrest as rival politicians, addressing large groups of electors, have attacked their opponent's policies and urged the people to vote for a new set of policies.

But there cannot have been many elections to compare with that of April 1831 for excitement. This was the second election to take place within a year—and what a year! In France, the middle classes had revolted, thrown the Bourbon King off the throne and replaced him with Louis Philippe. The Belgians had revolted against the Dutch and had created a new nation. Throughout Germany and the Austrian Empire there had been revolts led by students demanding political reform and supported by working classes demanding social reform.

In the south of England farmworkers rioted against low wages and smashed the new farm machinery which they thought was the cause of their conditions. Cobbett described the south as one gigantic blaze as ricks were burned, cattle maimed, machinery broken and houses attacked.

At this time the Tories had been in power for about fifty years when, in 1829–1830, they were suddenly thrown into a crisis. The Prime Minister—the highly respected Duke of Wellington—succeeded in offending first the liberal Tories, by refusing to grant Catholic Emancipation in 1827–1828, and then the Tories, by granting Emancipation in 1829. Liberal and die-hard Tories joined with the handful of Whigs to vote the government out of office and in July 1830 the King, William IV, asked Earl Grey to form a Whig government.

Was this the signal for a revolution, or could England escape the fate of France and other European countries? Could the unreformed, corruptly elected Parliament succeed in passing laws which would, amongst other things, mean the end of the power of the aristocracy?

Grey was one of the aristocratic Whigs who had continued to hold on to the ideas first put forward by Charles James Fox in the 1780s. In 1830 Grey was presented with the chance to show, in his own words, 'that in these days of democracy, it is possible to find real capacity in the high aristocracy'. Grey was no radical, anxious to change the face of England overnight; his government was composed almost entirely of members of the aristocracy; there were only three commoners in a Cabinet of thirteen.

Grey and the Whigs had been out of power for so long that they believed that the 'rules of the game' were stacked against them. How else could they explain the long years of Tory rule? If this was the case, then, thought Grey and his fellows, the 'rules' have to be changed.

O Cives: Cives.quærenda Pecunia primum est
Virtus post nummos.

The Laws.against Brib'ry Provision may make,
Yet means will be found both to give, and to take;
While Charms are in Flatt'ry, & Power in Gold,
Men will be Corrupted, and Liberty sold.

When a Candidate, Intrest is making for Votes,
How Cringing he seems to the arrantest Sots!
Dear Sir how d'ye do? –I am joyfull to see ye,
How fares your good Spouse? –& how goes y World

Can I serve you in any thing! –faith Sir I'll do't
If you'll be so kind as to give me your Vote.
Pray do me the Honour, an Ev'ning to pass
In Smoaking a Pipe and in taking a Glaß.

Away to the Tavern they quickly retire,
The Ploughman's Hail Fellow well met w.th y. Squire
Of his Company proud, he Huzza's & he drinks
And himself a great man of importance he thin

He struts w.th the Gold newly put in his Breeche
And dreams of vast Favours & mountains of
But as soon as the day of Election is over,
His wofull mistake he begins to discover;
The Squire is a Member – the Rustick who ch
Is now quite neglected – he no longer knows
Then Britons! betray not a Sordid vile Spir
Contemn Gilded Baits, & Elect Men of Merit

London Sold at the Print Shop in Grays Inn

The new Parliament met 28 Jan.y 1728.

13 *Ready Money, the Prevailing Candidate—or, the humours of an election,* 1727. In spite of various Acts against bribery, the practice continued well into the nineteenth century

New classes

Moreover, Grey and his Whigs recognised that England had changed during the previous sixty years or so. The growth of industrial towns grouped around factories had led to the growth of a new class of people. These were the rich middle class, who were helping to make England the workshop of the world. They realised their own economic importance and had been willing to leave politics to the aristocracy, provided that legislation was passed which helped them to get rich. They approved of Pitt's moves towards Free Trade; they welcomed the winning of an Empire in Canada, India and the West Indies; they

MR. MANGLES *respectfully requests those of his worthy Friends, who may be disposed to celebrate his return to Parliament by their own fire sides as on the last occasion to send the inclosed Dinner Ticket, on or before* THURSDAY *the 2d of* APRIL *next, to his Agent* MR. G. S. SMALLPEICE *who will in exchange for such Ticket, give the Bearer thereof an Order for*

TWELVE POUNDS OF BEEF,
ONE GALLON OF STRONG BEER,
TWO QUARTERN LOAVES,
THREE POUNDS AND A HALF OF FLOUR,
TWO POUNDS OF SUET,
TWO POUNDS OF RAISINS,
ONE POUND OF CURRANTS,
AND
TWO BOTTLES OF WINE, (PORT OR SHERRY).

MR. MANGLES *also begs respectfully to inform those Friends who may not be disposed to dine in public, and may not wish themselves to exchange the Dinner Ticket, that the same is transferrable to any of their Neighbors.*

An Answer is respectfully requested to be sent to MR. G. S. SMALLPEICE, on or before THURSDAY the 2nd of APRIL next.

14   Mr Mangles was at least honest about his bribery

supported the wars against France and Napoleon; they joined in the nation's praise of Nelson, Wellington, Pitt and other Tory leaders.

This situation lasted until 1815. There had been an increase in the population and the people who had crowded into the new towns to find work had to be fed. Foreign corn was cheap and could be brought into the country quite easily, but this meant that the English farmers could get less for their corn, and so could afford less rent for their farms. Many of the owners of the farms were aristocracy who sat in Parliament and so they passed the Corn Laws which ensured that no foreign corn could be imported until English corn had reached £4 a quarter ton.

15 *The Hustings at Covent Garden* painted by Charles Green. Until 1872 the voter had to go to the hustings (erected in the centre of the picture) and announce publicly the name of the candidate he was going to support. The electoral officer then marked the polling book while the rival gangs cheered or booed, sang or fought. This went on for as long as there were voters who still had not declared themselves—or for forty days, after which the election result was announced

This was a bitter blow to the middle class who were obliged to pay their workers higher wages, based on the price of bread. The Corn Laws were a blatant example of class legislation—they were intended to benefit only one class while harming every other.

While the Tories had not appreciated the change in society, the Whigs had as Brougham said: 'We don't live in the days of Barons—we live in the days of Leeds, of Bradford, of Halifax and Huddersfield. We live in the days when men are industrious and desire to be free.'

Macaulay, a leading Whig, speaking in the House of Commons during the debate on the Reform Bill said: 'History is full of revolutions, produced by causes similar to those which are now operating in England. A portion of the community which had been of no account expands and becomes strong. It demands a place in the system, suited . . . to its present power. If this is granted, all is well. If this is refused, then comes the struggle between the young energy of one class and the ancient privileges of another. Such is the struggle which the middle classes in

England are maintaining against an aristocracy ... or the owners of a ruined hovel, [who have] powers which are withheld from cities renowned ... for the marvels of their wealth and of their industry.'

Wellington and the Tories

In October 1830 Wellington declared: 'I have never read or heard of any measure ... which could satisfy my mind that the state of the representation could be improved. I am convinced that the country possesses ... a legislature which has the full and entire confidence of the country. The representation of the people at present contains a large body of the property of the country, in which the landed interests have a preponderating influence'.

The clue to Tory thinking lies in the last sentence; the Duke of Norfolk returned eleven members, Lord Lonsdale nine, Lord Darlington returned seven and many peers returned two or three—illustrating the Duke's point that the Constitution was founded on property, not on population, taxation or industry.

The Duke of Newcastle protested that 'my boroughs are mine to do what I like with', and agreed with the Duke of Wellington that the existing constitution

5 The British Lion, Britannia, King William IV and the 'angelic' Whigs drive the Duke of Cumberland, Wellington, Eldon, Wetherell and Croker into an outer darkness. The crowd cheers the destruction of the serpent, representing the rotten boroughs

was perfect. In further defence of the system the Tories pointed out that the old system had allowed for the emergence of Chatham and his son, Pitt the Younger, Fox, Burke and Canning, all of whom had been appointed by owners of rotten boroughs. Would a more democratic system have allowed these men to emerge, or would the only successful talent be that of mob oratory?

Grey, an aristocrat

Wellington and the Tories misjudged Grey as badly as they misjudged the spirit of the times. The times demanded reform, but Grey was no radical. It was his government which ordered the army to attack the agrarian rioters in 1830–1831; it was his Home Secretary, Lord Melbourne, who ordered the magistrates to get tough with arrested rioters and who later praised the magistrates at Tolpuddle for their attempt to nip trade unionism in the bud. Grey invited Lord John Russell to introduce the Reform Bills into Parliament and as Russell unfolded the Whig plan for reform, it became clear that really the proposed changes were minor indeed. Fifty-six boroughs with populations under 2,000 lost their representation altogether; thirty-one boroughs with populations of between 2,000 and 4,000 lost one of their MPs but kept one. Twenty-two new boroughs were created —fourteen of them in the industrial North and Midlands—with the privilege of returning two MPs, and twenty others were allowed to return one MP.

This did not do away with tiny boroughs altogether—Reigate had an electorate of only 152, and one hundred and fifteen MPs continued to sit for boroughs with an electorate of less than five hundred. Nor did it lead to equal representation when boroughs such as Tower Hamlets, in London, had over 7,000 voters on the roll. Huddersfield and Rochdale were new names on the electoral roll and this signified change; but not great change since most MPs continued to be elected by people in the South and West of the country.

Russell and the Bills

On 1 March 1831 Lord John introduced the first Reform Bill into the Commons. The debate was long and deep, passions ran high and added to the spirit of excitement in the country as a whole. Macaulay captured its spirit in a letter to a friend, when he described the last night of the debate:

> Such a scene as the division of last Tuesday I never saw, and never expect to see again. The crowd overflowed the House in every part. When the strangers were cleared out, and the doors locked, we had six hundred and eight members present ... The Ayes and Noes were like two volleys of cannon from opposite sides of a field of battle. When the opposition went out into the lobby, we spread ourselves over the benches on both sides of the House: When the doors were shut we began to speculate on our numbers. Everybody was desponding. We have lost. We are only two hundred and eighty at the most. They are three hundred ... As the tellers passed along our lowest row on the left hand side

the interest was insupportable—two hundred and ninety-one, two hundred and ninety-two. We were all standing up and stretching forward, telling with the tellers. At three hundred there was a short cry of joy, at three hundred and two another—suppressed however in a moment: for we did not yet know what the hostile force might be.

The doors were thrown open and in they came. Each of them, as he entered, brought some different report of their numbers . . . Alexander Barry told me that he had counted, and that they were three hundred and four. We were all breathless with anxiety, when Charles Wood, who stood near the door, jumped on a bench and cried out 'They are only three hundred and one.' We set up a shout that you might have heard to Charing Cross, waving our hats, stamping against the floor, and clapping our hands. The tellers scarcely got through the floor . . . But you might have heard a pin drop as Duncannon read the numbers. Then again the shouts broke out, and many of us shed tears. And the jaw of Peel fell, and the face of Twiss was as the face of a damned soul; and Herries looked like Judas taking his necktie off for the final operation.

But the rejoicing was short-lived. Although the representatives of the unreformed system had voted in favour of their own reform, when they got down to

27 The carrying of the second reading of the Reform Bill by a majority of one

discussing the Bill in detail they defeated the government's proposals by eight votes. In April 1831 Grey advised the King to dissolve Parliament so that the electorate could have a chance to show whether it supported Grey or Wellington.

18 *A Block on the Line*, 1867. Reform did not end in 1832, in spite of the hopes of 'Finality Jack', Lord Russell

A BLOCK ON THE LINE.

Superintendent Bull. "COME, LOOK ALIVE! I *MUST* HAVE THE RAIL CLEARED. THERE ARE NO END OF TRAINS DUE."
Johnny Russell. "IT'S MY JOB, SIR, IF YOU PLEASE."
John Bright. "*HIS* JOB! BEST LEAVE IT TO ME AND MY MATES."
Ben Dizzy. "OUR GANG'LL MANAGE IT, IF YOU'LL LEND A HAND, BILL GLADSTONE."

The election

Grey was supported by the radicals, the political unions, the working-class societies and others who favoured reform. His slogan and appeal was 'the Bill, the whole Bill, and nothing but the Bill'. Surprisingly, the lower classes demonstrated in favour of Grey's Bill—which was intended to do nothing for them. Indeed, by substituting the £10 household franchise for the many-sided franchises of the old system, the Bill set out to take away the vote from working-class electors in Preston, Westminster and other 'scot-and-lot' or 'pot-walloper' boroughs.

As was the case in most elections until 1886, most of the seats were not contested but the Whig government persuaded many borough patrons to return MPs who would support reform. Where elections were held the bribery and corruption was at a high level. The Tories spent over £400,000 on the election and complained that some electors stood out for 'as much as £10 before giving their pledge to support us'.

This election was, in one sense, a very simple one. Unlike most elections before and since, the electorate were asked to vote on one issue—the Bill. Indeed, the election was almost a referendum. The result was a blow for the Tories and a victory for the Whigs, because when Russell introduced his Bill on 24 June 1831 it was carried through the Commons by 136 votes; there were none of the scenes described by Macaulay: the Reformers had won the day.

Or had they? The Bill went to the Lords for their consideration and on 8 October 1831 the Lords threw out the Reform Bill by 199 votes to 158. This was the Tory backwoodsmen having their say; they refused to accept that England was changing. Outside Parliament riots seemed to be proving Macaulay's wisdom —if people can't get change in a peaceful way they will try to achieve it by more violent methods. The Duke of Newcastle was assaulted and his home attacked by the London mob; the windows of Wellington's house in Hyde Park were broken; the Duke of Cumberland was dragged from his horse on his way back from the House of Lords. There was rioting in Nottingham and Derby, Worcester and Bath, and on 29 October the city centre of Bristol was sacked by an angry mob in the worst riots of the year.

Russell had written: 'It is impossible that the whisper of a faction should prevail against the voice of the nation'. He decided to put his belief to the test and on 12 December 1931 he introduced his Reform Bill for the third time. This time the Commons supported him by a majority of 162 votes. The question was, what would the Lords do? On 7 May 1832 the Lords defeated the government and Grey resigned.

William IV

At first William IV had promised Grey that if necessary he would create enough new Peers to ensure that the Bill would pass the Lords. But he had become increasingly afraid that once moves were begun towards reform, the people would be encouraged to take the law into their own hands and depose the King and the aristocracy, as had happened in the French Revolution less than fifty years before. He asked Wellington to try to form a government and for a week Wellington and his friends tried to win enough support in the Commons but they failed, and on 14 May 1832 Grey agreed to William IV's appeal to become Prime Minister again.

The Lords, recognising that they could not stand out against the people and the King, and seeing that their leader could not form a government, finally gave in and in June the Reform Bill passed the Lords by 102 votes to 22—the majority of Tories abstaining, fearing a 'swamping' by new Liberal Peers more than the Reform Bill.

Result of this election

A writer in the *Poor Man's Guardian*, 25 October 1832, appreciated that the Reform Act and the surrounding elections had changed very little. He wrote: 'The promoters of the Reform Bill projected it, not with a view to subvert, or even remodel our aristocratic institutions, but to consolidate them by a reinforcement of sub-aristocracy from the middle classes . . . The only difference between the Whigs and the Tories is this—the Whigs would give the shadow to preserve the substance; the Tories would not give the shadow, because stupid as they are, the millions will not stop at shadows but proceed onwards to realities.'

This is, of course, precisely what Macaulay had hoped for when he asked the Commons to accept reform in place of revolution. In fact, the aristocracy continued to dominate English economic, social and political life right up to the end of the nineteenth century.

The election of 1784 had established the right of the Prime Minister to ask for a dissolution of Parliament whenever he thought he might win the support of the people. The elections of 1831 established the right of the government to expect the Lords to accept the Commons' decision on important matters, and confirmed that the King had the duty to agree to a Prime Minister's request to create enough Peers to ensure that this would be done. In 1831–1832 Grey did not have to carry out his threat because the Lords finally agreed to accept the Reform Bill. In 1911 the Lords again threatened to hold up a Reform Bill, and again, the Prime Minister, Asquith, had to use the threat of new creations to persuade the diehards to change their minds (Chapter 6).

In the wilderness

In Chapter 2 we saw that the Tory party was split between 1828 and 1830 over the question of Catholic Emancipation. One result of this was that the Whigs were able to pass the Reform Act, 1832. For the next thirty years—until 1865—the Tories were rarely in office; Peel held office between 1841 and 1846, while Lord Derby led minority Tory governments for short periods in 1852 and 1859.

Why did the Tories do so badly? In the first place they suffered because of the utterances of the more die-hard members of the Party; when some urged that the Reform Bill was a betrayal of all that was good in England, it is not surprising that the moderate, middle-class voter should decide to vote for the Whigs. The opinions of these reactionaries did not reflect the policies which Peel, Derby, Disraeli or other leaders would have put into practice if only they had won power. But the electorate was not to know that; just as many moderate voters in the 1920s believed that a vote for Labour was a vote for Russia (Chapter 7), so, in the middle of the nineteenth century, many people believed that a vote for a Tory was a vote for the Corn Laws, Game Laws, Peterloo Massacres and so on.

Then again the Tories suffered a disaster in 1846 when Peel and the majority of the Cabinet voted to repeal the Corn Laws while Disraeli led a backbencher's revolt against this betrayal of the interests of the landowner and farmer. The better-known, more intelligent Peelites finally joined hands with the Whigs, both Aberdeen and Gladstone becoming Peelite Prime Ministers of Whig-Liberal governments. This blow to the Tories is illustrated by the story that when Wellington was being told the names of the members of Derby's Tory government (1852) he kept on saying, 'Who? Who?' and the government became known as the 'who-who' government.

Disraeli

Having led the revolt against Peel, Disraeli became a leader of the small band of Tory MPs although he did not try to act as leader of the Tory party. He left that post to Lord George Bentinck and later to Lord Derby. He appreciated that his Jewish background, his lack of landed wealth and his uncertain political past —he had been a Whig and a radical before becoming a Tory MP—would have made it difficult for the noble aristocrats, the squires and the backwoodsmen to accept him as Party Leader.

Disraeli acted as a leader, explaining his Party's policy to the new electorate and trying to persuade the Party's chiefs to drop the policies which labelled them 'reactionary'. However, he had little chance of success until, in 1865, Palmerston

19 *The Election*, 1857. This shows the hustings with the candidates and their friends. Few of the crowd had the right to vote but they enjoyed the flavour of the election and the bribes of the various candidates. The patriotic cry for 'Pam' (Lord Palmerston) and the British Lion, appealed to the jingoistic crowd; Disraeli's task was to turn this into a Tory appeal

died and Russell became the aged leader of the Liberal Party with Gladstone as his chief lieutenant and heir-apparent.

Both Russell and Gladstone were convinced that a further dose of Parliamentary reform was required in the Britain which had progressed economically and socially since 1832. Russell had become convinced that the lower middle classes and the well-paid skilled workers should get a vote. Robert Lowe, who had been in Palmerston's government as a colleague of Russell's and Gladstone's, opposed the Liberal leaders' attempts to introduce a new Reform Bill.

Disraeli and reform

Disraeli had no difficulty in persuading the Tories to support Lowe in opposing Gladstone and Russell and in June 1866 Russell resigned. At the end of June the Queen invited Derby to form a government.

The main question facing the Tory government was that of reform. Disraeli first thought it might be a good idea, in alliance with the reforming Liberals, to pass Gladstone's Bill. However, he realised that this would only help to make Gladstone appear a Liberal reformer who could drive even the Tories to do what he wanted.

In the end he decided to bring in a Tory Reform Bill which went much further than Gladstone had intended to go, because it gave the vote to every male householder in the boroughs and also redistributed seats so that the larger towns got a fairer representation than they had been given in 1832. This Reform Act (1867) was a surprising development since it was proposed by a Tory government which had opposed a lesser reform proposed by Gladstone and Russell.

His Reform Act added about 3 million voters to the electoral rolls but when Disraeli (Prime Minister after Derby's retirement) called for an election in April 1868 he found that these were still unwilling to trust the Tories, who won only 279 seats compared with the 379 won by Gladstone's Liberals.

Disraeli and party reform

In opposition Disraeli was careful not to oppose the Gladstone government on every count. He realised that the country needed a good deal of modernising reform if it was to be able to cope with the many problems of the late nineteenth century. Many of these reforms were long overdue and had only been postponed

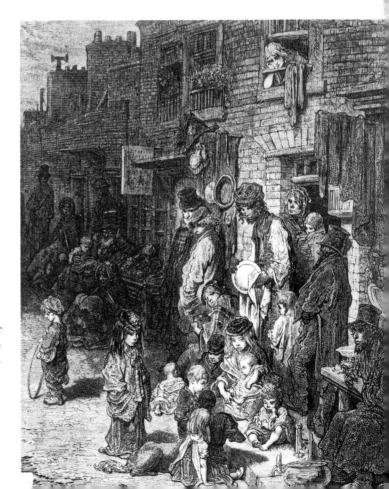

20 *Wentworth Street, Whitechapel* by Doré. None of these people had a vote in 1872 when this picture was drawn, and the politicians did little, if anything, for them

BOROUGH AND COUNTY ELECTIONS.

MESSRS. DENTON AND GRAY

Intimate to their Workmen that they are at perfect
liberty to Vote for any Candidate they please, and
that the side they take in Politics will not in any
way affect their employment.

Middleton Ship Yard.
Hartlepool. June 23rd. 1868.

Hartlepool: J. Procter, Printer and Lithographer by Steam Power. H.745.

21 Under the open system of voting, the voter had to pay attention to the wishes of his employer
and other people of influence. Landowners could control the voting pattern of their tenants,
contractors could influence people eager to get a contract or a job

because of the long domination of English politics by Palmerston, one of whose
favourite sayings was 'You can't keep adding to the statute book year after year'.
Because of this attitude the country had not reformed its civil service, army,
judicial system, trade union movement or educational system as it should have
done.

Disraeli allowed Gladstone a more-or-less free hand from 1868 to 1872, much
to the disappointment of his followers who had hoped that the Tories would
oppose these reforms and make life difficult for the Liberals. He turned to the
question of organising his now stronger political party. He founded the Conservative Central Office (1868), and appointed John Gorst as Principal Agent of the
Tory Party with instructions to strengthen the party organisation in the country
as a whole. One proof of Gorst's success lies in the many uncontested elections
of 1868 and 1874; well over half the seats were not contested in both these elections,
but whereas in 1868 the Liberals had been chosen in 213 uncontested elections
while the Tories had been given only 116, in 1874 Gorst managed to get 178
walkovers for the Tories while conceding only 150 to the Liberals.

Disraeli and patriotism

In matters of foreign policy Palmerston had exhibited the self-righteous attitudes
which have since become strongly associated with the Victorian era, claiming
that 'the strong arm of England' should protect British subjects, even if this meant
interfering in the affairs of other countries. Gladstone's attitude was quite the
reverse, for he believed in 'equality of the weak and the strong' and declared
that we should not meddle in the internal policies of other States, just as we should
not expect them to meddle in ours.

Disraeli attacked Gladstone's lack of foreign and imperial ambition in a speech made at the Crystal Palace in 1872, during which he said that the working classes of England were conservatives in the purest and best sense; by which he meant, he said, that they 'are proud of belonging to a great country, and wish to maintain its greatness; that they are proud of belonging to an Imperial country, and are resolved to maintain, if they can, their Empire.'

Proof that Disraeli spoke for the British lower classes in their national pride and hatred of the foreigner, is supplied by the music hall song popular in the mid-1870s:

> He hungered for his victim, he's pleased when blood is shed,
> But let us hope his crimes may recoil on his own head.
> We don't want to fight but *by jingo* if we do,
> We've got the ships, we've got the men,
> And we've got the money too.
> We've fought the bear before, and while we're Britons true,
> The Russians shall not have Constantinople.

Disraeli the moderate

While Disraeli was reorganising his party so that it was better fitted to fight the next election, and whipping up support among the lower classes by his appeal to their 'jingoism', he was careful not to oppose Gladstone's much needed reforms. But in 1872 he began to sense that the British people were tired of this meddlesome, though necessary legislation. He said: 'As time advanced it was not difficult

22 *A Jew Voting*, painted by S. Begg. The polling booths can be seen in the background. In 1872 the Ballot Act was passed, to end the open system of voting and to establish the modern method of secret voting

to perceive that extravagance was being substituted for energy by the government. The unnatural stimulus was subsiding. Their paroxysms ended in prostration. Some took refuge in melancholy, and their eminent chief alternated between a menace and a sigh. As I sat opposite the Treasury Bench the Ministers reminded me of one of those marine landscapes not very uncommon on the coasts of South America. You behold a range of exhausted volcanoes. Not a flame flickers on a single pallid crest. But the situation is still dangerous. There are occasional earthquakes, and ever and anon the dark rumbling of the sea.'

The description 'extinct volcanoes' was a telling one which stuck. It helped to remind the voters how troublesome the government had been and how dangerous the Liberals might yet become if their leaders listened to Chamberlain with his Republican talk of abolishing the monarchy. This appeal to the voter to 'Vote Tory and escape Liberal legislation' was calculated to appeal to the middle classes who had once looked to the Liberals as their rightful representatives but now began to believe that Liberalism was radicalism, while Toryism was safety.

The rich landed aristocrat had usually been a Tory; Gladstone and Disraeli between them made Tories out of the rich middle class.

Disraeli the reformer

But Disraeli could not hope to be elected on a negative 'we don't want Gladstone' vote. He also wanted to appear as a social reformer. Speaking at Manchester in 1872, he said:

I am not here to maintain that there is nothing to be done to increase the well-being of the working classes of this country; but in attempting to legislate upon social matters the great object is to be practical—to have before us some distinct aims and some distinct means by which they can be accomplished.

I think public attention as regards these matters ought to be concentrated upon sanitary legislation ... pure air, pure water, the inspection of unhealthy habitations, the adulteration of food; these and many kindred matters may be legitimately dealt with by the legislature ... A great scholar and a great wit ... said that in his opinion there was a great mistake in the *Vulgate*, which as you all know is the Latin translation of the Holy Scriptures and that, instead of saying 'Vanity of Vanities, all is Vanity'—*Vanitas Vanitatum, omnia vanitas*—the wise and witty king really said *Sanitas sanitatum omnia sanitas*. It is impossible to over-rate the importance of the subject. After all, the first consideration of a minister should be the health of the people ... the country may be famous in the annals and actions of the world, but if the population every ten years decreases, and the stature of the race every ten years diminishes, the history of that country will soon be the history of the past.

When this idea was attacked by the Liberals, Disraeli returned to the subject at his Crystal Palace speech a little later in 1872: 'Now what is the feeling upon these subjects of the Liberal Party? A leading member ... denounced them the

23 *Benjamin Bombastes*, a reflection of Disraeli's claim to have replaced Palmerston as the 'patriot'. Disraeli is challenging anyone to displace the boots, representing British interests

other day as "the policy of sewage". Well it may be "the policy of sewage" to a Liberal Member of Parliament. But to one of the labouring multitude of England, who has found fever always to be one of the inmates of his household . . . it is a question of life and death.'

The election

On Saturday 24 January 1874 Disraeli was staying at Edward's Hotel in London, planning to buy a new house. He was amazed when he read in the *Times* that Gladstone had decided to ask the Queen to dissolve Parliament and to hold an election. Gladstone's platform was 'the abolition of income-tax'; by Monday, Disraeli and his chief assistants had got their platform out in time for that day's papers. He emphasised the meddlesome nature of the Liberal legislation, promised less of this when the Tories were returned, and argued that it was time that Britain took a more active line abroad.

The election was the first to be held after the passing of the Ballot Act, 1872 (which replaced the system of open voting by secret ballot) and it was in comparison with former occasions 'a quiet election'. With employers unable to check on how their workers voted and landowners unable to control the votes of their tenants, it was the first 'fair' election. One result of this was the sweeping gain made by the Irish Nationalists who won 57 seats in Ireland—mainly at the expense of the Liberals.

But for Gladstone the election was significant because of the surprising result.

24 *Mosé in Egitto*. The extension of British influence into Egypt and other parts of Africa was part of Tory policy, popular with the electorate and opposed by the pacific Liberals. Disraeli is represented as Moses

Disraeli and his Tories won 352 seats to Gladstone's 243 seats; even counting the 57 Irish Nationalists as allies to the Liberals, Disraeli had an overall majority in the Commons. The Tories were back again after nearly 30 years in the wilderness.

The long-term results

Disraeli's success confirmed his belief that the Tory line should be empire, monarchy and national pride. From this time on the Tories became the 'patriotic party'—a role they could never have hoped to fill if Palmerston had lived or if the Liberals had followed Palmerston's policies.

For the Tories this election ushered in a golden age. Whereas they had been in the wilderness for about 30 years since 1846, for the thirty years after 1874 they were in office for all except 7 years and became, in a real sense, the 'governing party'.

Gladstone in trouble 1880–1885

At the general election of 1880 Disraeli's Tories were defeated and Gladstone became Prime Minister for the second time. This second Ministry has been called 'the Ministry of All Troubles' because Gladstone seemed to face one difficulty after another. In 1881–1882 he was forced, against his better judgment and against the spirit of Liberalism, to occupy Egypt in order to safeguard British investment there. This, in turn, led him to send Gordon to Khartoum to bring out the British diplomats and their families under attack from a religious fanatic, the Mahdi. When Gordon was murdered in 1884, Gladstone was blamed by the Tories and by the country at large for having failed to send a relieving force;

25   The Central Lobby of the House of Commons, 1886. From left to right: Inspector Denning, Hillman (a clerk), John Bright, Sir William Harcourt, Gosset (Deputy Sergeant), Labouchere, Bradlaugh, Chamberlain, Parnell, Gladstone, Randolph Churchill, Hartington, Chaplin, Leveson–Gower, Spencer, Lord Hill, Mr Hansard

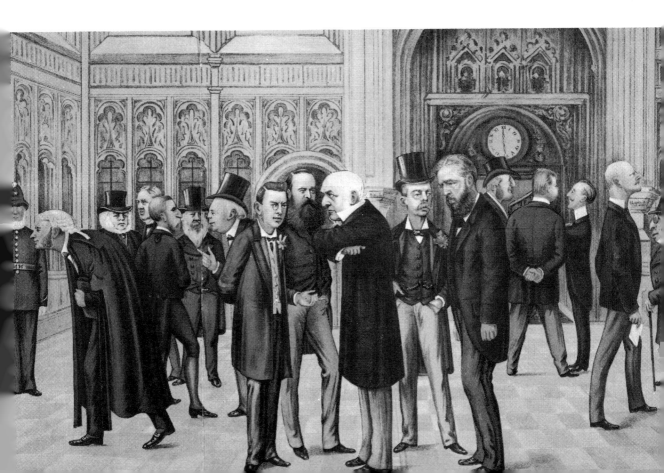

26 *The Bag-Fox*, 1884. The extension of the franchise in 1885 was preceded by the Act which changed the boundaries of most constituencies. Seats were redistributed so that the more densely-populated towns gained fairer representation in the Commons

whereas he had been known as the G(rand) O(ld) M(an), the newspapers now christened him G(ordon's) O(wn) M(urderer).

Disraeli's active policies in South Africa had led to the occupation of the Transvaal where the Dutch Boers had emigrated from the Cape; Gladstone had opposed this occupation but found himself in charge of a government which first fought the Boers who wanted independence and then—after a defeat—retreated, allowing the Boers to govern themselves again. Here again, he had the worst of both worlds. He lost the support of the Liberals for having fought against the 'gallant Boers' and he lost the support of the 'patriots' by withdrawing after a defeat.

In the Commons he was under constant attack from a small group of Tories led by Lord Randolph Churchill; this 'fourth party' used every excuse to attack Gladstone and his policies. The only important measure which he was able to get through the Commons was the Third Reform Act which increased the electorate by about 2 million, since it extended the household suffrage to adult males living in county constituencies. This 1884 Reform required a redistribution of constituencies and this Act passed through the Commons in 1885.

Ireland and its problems

Gladstone had first come to power in 1868, saying: 'My mission is to pacify Ireland'. In his second ministry, 1880–1885, he continued to try to find solutions to the Irish problem; but whatever he tried seemed doomed to fail. The generous Land Act, 1881 was opposed by Parnell, leader of the Irish Nationalist Party in the Commons and the 'uncrowned king of Ireland' outside Parliament. When Gladstone had Parnell arrested and imprisoned in Kilmainham Gaol, the problems of Ireland loomed even larger. Riots, burning, cattle maiming and other outrages convinced Gladstone that the Irish problem required a political solution and not merely a series of Land Acts. Chamberlain, a leading member of Gladstone's Cabinet, proposed that the Irish should be given some sort of local self-government with county and borough councils, based on the English model. This did not satisfy the Irish Party, who wanted complete self-government; their cry was 'Home Rule for Ireland'. In 1885 Parnell united with the Tories in the Commons to defeat Gladstone's budget and 'the Ministry of All Troubles' came to an end.

1885 election

The Liberal campaign in this election ran on two lines. On the one hand there was the radical programme put forward by Joseph Chamberlain and his supporters. Speaking at Hull in August 1885 Chamberlain said: 'Everywhere in the county I see a quickening of political life; everywhere there is discussion and hope and expectation. Gentlemen, it will be dangerous to disappoint that hope. It will be impossible to stifle that discussion; and if there are any people who imagine that the enfranchisement of two millions of citizens can have taken place, and that these men intend to make no use of the privilege which has been conferred upon them, they will have a rude awakening . . . I have always had a deep conviction that when the people came to govern themselves the social evils which disgrace our civilisation would at last find a hearing and a remedy . . . I do not want you to think that I suggest to you that Legislation can accomplish all that we desire . . . [But] I want you not to accept as final or as perfect, arrangements under which millions of your fellow-countrymen are subject to untold privations and misery, with the evidence all around them of accumulated wealth and unbounded luxury . . .'.

Speaking at Warrington in September, he admitted 'this is Socialism . . . Of course it is Socialism. The greater part of municipal work is Socialism, and every kindly act of legislation by which the community has sought to discharge its responsibilities and its obligations to the poor is Socialism, but it is none the worse for that. Our object is the elevation of the poor, of the masses of the people'.

On the other hand there was the old-fashioned Liberal programme put forward by Gladstone with its emphasis on lowering income tax. Speaking in October, Gladstone attacked the Chamberlain programme: 'there is a disposition to think that the government ought to do this and that, and that the government ought to do everything . . . If the government takes into its hand that which the man ought to do for himself, it will inflict upon him greater mischiefs than all the benefits he will have received . . . the spirit of self-reliance should be preserved in the minds of the masses of the people, in the minds of every member of that class'.

Chamberlain was no respecter of persons, not even of the person of Mr Gladstone, the venerable leader of the Party. He declared: 'it is therefore perfectly futile and ridiculous for any political Rip Van Winkle to come down from the mountain on which he has been slumbering, and to tell us that these things are to be excluded from the Liberal programme'.

Parnell and the Irish Nationalists were confident of winning most of the Irish seats; they concentrated most of their attention on trying to persuade the Catholics

43

27 (*left*) Gladstone introducing the Second Home Rule Bill in the House of Commons, 1893

28 (*below*) the declaration of the result of the poll outside the Town Hall, Leeds, where Gladstone's son, Herbert, upheld the family name

in England, Wales and Scotland to vote Tory, since Lord Randolph Churchill had told Parnell that the Tories might consider Home Rule for Ireland.

The election result was a stalemate; the Liberals won 334 seats, the Tories 250, while the Irish Nationalists with their 86 seats held the balance between the two major parties. When Salisbury announced that he was not ready to support Home Rule, Parnell took his Irish Party into the lobbies with the Liberals and Gladstone became Prime Minister for the third time in 1886.

Gladstone was out of touch with the spirit of his time, as much as the Tories had been in the 1820s (Chapter 2). Chamberlain had a much better idea of what was wanted of a Liberal government when he talked about social improvements. But Gladstone, without consulting any of his colleagues, announced that he intended to bring in a Home Rule Bill. Chamberlain realised that this would mean a bitter fight in Parliament, the hostility of the imperially-minded electorate, and little or no chance of getting any of his socialist programme on the statute book. He was in any case exasperated with the Old Man, and felt that he could lead a modernised Liberal Party in a more radical direction if only he could push Gladstone into retirement.

On the other hand there were the few remaining Whigs, who felt that under Gladstone, Liberalism had become altogether too radical as compared with the Whig-Liberalism of Palmerston. Under the leadership of Lord Hartington, a number of these die-hards joined forces with Chamberlain and his supporters to defeat the Home Rule Bill in the House of Commons in 1886.

The Orange Card, 1886

Gladstone resigned and called for another general election in July 1886. Here, as in 1831, the electorate was asked to vote on a single issue—in this case the issue was Home Rule for Ireland. Chamberlain and the Liberals urged the electorate to reject this, so that Parliament could get on with more important social reforms. The Tories' main speaker in this election was Lord Randolph Churchill, who had promised Parnell a Tory Home Rule Bill. Now he led the campaign against Gladstone. Speaking to the electors of South Paddington in 1886, Churchill declared:

> Mr Gladstone has reserved for his closing days a conspiracy against the honour of Britain and the welfare of Ireland . . . [more base] than any of those other numerous designs and plots which, during the last century, have occupied his imagination . . . For the sake of this nonsense . . . all business other than that is to be suspended . . . all useful and deserved reforms are to be indefinitely postponed, the British Constitution is to be torn up. And why? For this reason and no other: to gratify the ambition of an old man in a hurry . . . [who] now stands before the country all alone, rejected by a democratic House of Commons.

Appealing to the Protestants of Ireland, Churchill urged them to resist Home

45

Rule, and in particular he asked the Protestants of Ulster to prepare to fight the Old Man's proposals. If, by any chance, Gladstone did push his Bill through Parliament, said Churchill, the Protestants of the North of Ireland should arm themselves and undertake a civil war with the Gladstone government. In a striking phrase Churchill said: 'Ulster will fight, and Ulster will be right'. This Protestant appeal won many working-class votes for the Tories in British constituencies where Irish immigrants were as unwelcome as coloured immigrants were to be in the 1960s and 1970s. Churchill played on this working-class antipathy for the immigrant, and his Party benefited.

The propertied classes also opposed Gladstone's Irish policies; the working class felt that Home Rule was a betrayal of Britain's imperial greatness whilst the propertied middle class felt that Gladstone's previous Irish policies had been all wrong. He had taken the Anglican Church funds and divided them among the Irish population at large; he had compelled landowners to sell their property to their tenant farmers. This interference with property alarmed the landowning class but also disturbed the middle classes who, although they did not own land in Ireland, had a respect for property. If Gladstone could do this for the landed aristocrat what might he not do for the industrial, commercial and house property of the middle class?

The election result

In July the country went to the polls and in a major landslide the Tories won 394 seats (including 78 won by the Liberal Unionists led by Chamberlain), while the Liberals won only 191 seats. Even with the 86 votes of the Irish Nationalists against them the Tories had a majority in the House of Commons and Lord Salisbury became Prime Minister once again.

One of the main results of this election was to quicken the process by which the main political parties were becoming class parties. In general the Tories had always been the party of the landed aristocrat; now they also became the party of the middle class, while the Liberals became the party of the less well-off. This was a bonus for the Tories but a danger for the Liberals; what sort of policies were Liberals to follow if they wanted to keep the support of the less well-off? Could the Liberals produce a set of reforming policies which would satisfy this class without frightening off the remaining middle-class Liberals? If not, where would the lower classes look for solutions to their grievances?

Some of the lower classes, of course, had always looked to the Tories—as their natural leaders, as the guardians of their Anglican religion against the Nonconformist Liberals, as the upholders of Britain's imperial greatness and now, as the Protestant bulwark against the Catholic plot of Home Rule. 'Home Rule,' said Churchill, 'is Rome Rule' and the lower-class Protestants of the English, Welsh and Scottish industrial towns were not going to have that.

There are two interesting 'ifs' connected with this election: if Chamberlain had managed to persuade Gladstone to accept his socialist policy, would the

29 The Duke of Devonshire speaking in the Lords, February 1892. The Lords had become a Conservative stronghold as a result of opposition to Gladstone's policies—particularly his Irish policy

Labour Party ever have been founded? If, again, Parliament had accepted Gladstone's Home Rule proposals, would we have had the Ulster problem of the 1970s? In a sense, we who live nearly a hundred years after this 1886 election, are still living with its results.

5   1906: The People into Parliament

Permanent Tory rule?

We have already seen in Chapter 3 that Disraeli's major contribution to the Tory Party was to give it the appearance of being the 'patriotic' or 'national' party, and one result was that the Tories governed the country for most of the period 1874–1906. Gladstone had his 'Ministry of All Troubles', his brief Home Rule Ministry (Chapter 4), and he was Prime Minister again in 1892. But this Liberal government fell apart after his retirement in 1893 as the Liberals quarrelled over policies, the leadership, Ireland and other problems. In 1895 the Tories resumed what seemed, to many, their rightful role as governors.

An election took place in 1900 following belated British success in the Boer War; in the mass hysteria which seized the country on such news as the relief of Mafeking, nationalist, war-making Tories won a resounding success. The Liberals, on the other hand, were torn even further apart by the effects of the war. Some sympathised with the imperialist attitude, and, led by Lord Rosebery, they supported Tory policy; the other faction—including Lloyd George—opposed the Tory war against the 'gallant Boers', and suffered from attacks in newspapers and cartoons. Members also faced physical attacks, such as that on Lloyd George when he went to speak in Birmingham, a stronghold of imperialism.

It went almost unnoticed that in this election two Labour MPs were returned, and few people noticed that in 1900 a meeting had taken place at the Memorial Hall, Farringdon Street, London, between the representatives of the various socialist societies (the Fabians, the Independent Labour Party, the Social Democratic Federation) and representatives of the trade union movement. The Labour Representation Committee formed at that meeting changed its name to the Labour Party in 1906, and modern British politics had been born.

Tory misrule

Lord Salisbury retired from office in 1902 and was succeeded by his nephew, Arthur Balfour; the landed aristocracy may have appeared to give away power to the middle classes in 1832 (Chapter 2) but they certainly held on to the reality of power and leadership well into this century. But Balfour's ministry was never as confident or sure as that of his uncle. By 1903 the Tory government was visibly falling apart, and a campaign to get rid of Balfour was organised under the slogan 'Balfour Must Go' (or BMG for short). A party which is uncertain of its leader is unlikely to present a confident face to the electorate (as the Labour Party discovered in the 1950s when controversies over Hugh Gaitskell's leadership helped

30 The title page of the paper edited by Keir Hardie

Harold Macmillan and the Tories to win the 1959 election against what seemed to be overwhelming odds—see Chapter 9).

One reason for this leadership problem was the presence and the policies of Joseph Chamberlain; having split the Liberals in 1886, Chamberlain had become the darling of the Tory Party with his Imperialist policy after he became Colonial Secretary in 1895. He accepted responsibility for the outbreak of the Boer War and, while becoming the bitter enemy of Lloyd George and other pro-Boers, he became the idol of the Tories and the patriots. But when Salisbury retired, Chamberlain felt that the Tory Party should take a more active policy in peacetime; in particular, he felt that it was time the country gave up its policy of Free Trade—by which there were no import duties levied on imports into Britain. Like every other country in the world, she should impose tariffs (or import duties) on foreign goods so as to make them more expensive and less able to compete with British goods in the home market.

Tariff Reform

Chamberlain was conscious of the mass of the electorate. He realised that Britain was no longer the workshop of the world, that Germany and the USA had become stronger industrial powers, taking away many of Britain's former markets as well

31 (*left*) a Liberal poster of 1906 with attacks on the billposter, Balfour

32 (*right*) a Liberal poster of 1906. The soldier asks 'Is *this* what we fought for?

as establishing many of their products on the British home market. Chamberlain saw that one result of this was the continuing high level of unemployment; this was a new and disturbing feature of British life. There had always been some unemployment as machinery replaced manpower but never, until the end of the nineteenth century, had there been this large-scale and continuing unemployment, with twelve per cent of trade union members unemployed in the 1890s.

Chamberlain believed that if the country protected its own industries against foreign competition this would help to increase the sales of British goods at home and so create employment. He also hoped to use British tariffs as a bargaining tool with the independent members of the British Empire—Australia, Canada and New Zealand. These countries had their own systems of tariffs against foreign goods—which included those from Britain. Chamberlain believed that it should be possible to work out a scheme by which the colonies put a lower tariff on British goods than on goods from other countries if, in return, Britain put a lower tariff on colonial goods than on goods from elsewhere. This system, to be known as 'Imperial Preference', would give Britain a larger share of colonial markets and so lead to even more employment in British factories.

The Empire and defence

It would also knit the Empire more closely together in a sort of Imperial Common Market; while Britain would benefit, the colonies also would gain since they would have a guaranteed access to the British domestic market for their grain, wool, lamb and other products which would be cheaper than the more heavily tariffed goods from Denmark and other countries. The colonies were producing many raw materials which Britain needed, whilst British industries produced many of the manufactured goods which the less-developed colonies could not make for themselves.

Such a closely knit Empire would also be a permanent threat to the German attempt to dominate the world. Chamberlain had tried to persuade the new Kaiser, Wilhelm II of Germany, to listen to reason and join an Anglo-Saxon alliance of Britain, Germany and the USA. The Kaiser was as unwilling to join as were the Americans; both suspected the British of wanting to maintain their own leading position by preventing other countries (Germany and the USA) from expanding as the British had done in the nineteenth century. The warlike policies of the Germans must, Chamberlain believed, one day lead to a clash with Britain, which would need the support of her Empire if she were to defeat a powerful Germany.

The Liberals reunite

The Liberals were in disarray after 1900; they stood by, helplessly, while the return of the troops from their victories over the Boers confirmed the public opinion that 'to be Tory is to be British'. But in 1902 the Tories presented the Liberals with a chance to reunite and to appeal to a strong section of the electorate. Balfour was responsible for the 1902 Education Act which, among other things, compelled Local Education Authorities to pay towards the maintenance of Catholic and Anglican Schools. The Nonconformists rallied to the slogan 'Rome on the Rates' and up and down the country ratepayers went to gaol rather than pay towards the church schools. In general the Nonconformists were Liberal in outlook, disliking the Anglican Church which was once described as 'the Tory Party at prayer', almost as much as they hated Rome and its Church.

The campaign against the Education Act failed to defeat the Tory policy but it did serve to rally many people to the Liberal cause. When, in 1903, Chamberlain came forward with his Tariff Reform policy the Liberals leapt at the chance of attracting more support. They argued that this was a betrayal of half a century of history; that Britain had been great only because of Free Trade; that Tariff Reform would lead to higher prices at home—for manufactured goods and food. In particular, they made a big issue out of the price of Free Trade bread and Tariff Reform bread, arguing that the housewives would pay for Tory policy.

Chinese slavery

As with so many things, 'nothing fails like failure'. The Tories were split by Tariff Reform; Chamberlain and the Duke of Devonshire resigned from the Cabinet and Chamberlain took his case to the country in a series of monster meetings. Most Tories refused to go along with him but the electorate saw a divided party and, as the history of the Labour Party was to prove 'divided we fall'. To fill the cup of Tory discontent an issue was made of 'Chinese Slavery'. Mine owners in South Africa brought in thousands of Chinese to work in their mines; in order to ensure that these immigrants did not run away or go to work for a rival, they had to sign a document which bound them to a particular owner for seven years, during which they had to live in the compound provided by the mine, repay the cost of transport from China to Africa and, in general, be tied to the owner. This was not slavery by any stretch of the imagination, but a hostile Press, an invigorated Liberal Party and a Nonconformist conscience already roused over Free Trade and the Education Act, seized on yet another opportunity of making life difficult for the Tory government which allowed this to happen in South Africa.

'Is this what they died for?' was the question attached to cartoons showing scenes from the recent Boer War, set alongside scenes of Chinese coolies being chained to a mine owner. The War had been the main cause of the Tory success in 1900; by 1906 people had had time to have second thoughts about a war fought for gold and diamonds, against a small nation that merely wanted to be left alone. They also began to have doubts about a government which had taken so long to defeat the untrained armies put into the field by the Boer farmers, and about the barbaric methods of concentration camps invented by Kitchener as the only way in which the Boers could finally be defeated.

The Irish

Gladstone and the Liberals had tried twice to get Parliament to pass a Home Rule Bill. In 1886 Chamberlain and other Liberals had defeated the Bill in the Commons (Chapter 4); in 1893 Gladstone persuaded the Commons to pass a Home Rule Bill, only to have it defeated in the Lords, now a bastion of Toryism. By 1906 Parnell had died and been replaced by John Redmond as leader of the Irish Nationalists, still anxious for Home Rule, still hoping that the Liberals would remain true to the old cause. Redmond campaigned throughout Britain asking the Irish to vote Liberal at the next election.

Labour

In 1900 the Labour Representation Committee was supported by only a handful of the weaker trade unions. Most of the older, stronger unions, for skilled workers, preferred to trust the Liberals to represent them and their interests. In 1901, however, they were made to think again. The Chairman of the Taff Vale Railway Company prosecuted the Amalgamated Society of Railway Servants for damages

33 Conservative Prime Minister Arthur Balfour, at an election meeting, December 1905. The Conservative defeat in this election led to demands for Balfour's resignation—nobody loves a loser—and he was replaced by Bonar Law

done to his railway company during a strike called by the Union in 1899. To most people's surprise the courts decided that the Union had to pay; on an appeal to the House of Lords, Britain's final Court of Appeal, the Law Lords fixed the damages at £23,000 and compelled the Union to pay £19,000 in costs as well.

After this no trade union could call a strike without facing the possibility of being sued for damages by the employer. The old unions asked Balfour's government to pass a new Trade Union Act to make unions safe from such claims, but Balfour, with remarkable blindness, failed to do so and the unions which had once ignored the infant Labour Party now joined it in the hope that this Party would be able to exert some influence in Parliament. These skilled unions brought a good deal to the Labour Party—large funds to support electoral campaigns and to pay Labour MPs if elected; strong organisations able to provide a working-class vote in many constituencies; capable leaders accustomed to negotiating with employers and able to give an account of themselves at election meetings; and able candidates to stand at elections.

pact, 1903

In 1903 the secretary of this Party was a young Scotsman, Ramsay MacDonald. He approached the Liberal Chief Whip—Herbert Gladstone—and suggested that both Labour and Liberal Parties had much in common. They both disliked the Tariff Reform campaign, they were both opposed to the 1902 Education Act, to Chinese Slavery and to the Taff Vale decision. MacDonald suggested that it would be a waste of votes if Labour and Liberal candidates stood in the same constituencies, so dividing the anti-Tory voters and perhaps allowing the Tories to be elected on a minority vote.

By the electoral pact between these two, both promised to use their influence to persuade local parties and associations to withdraw candidates in certain constituencies and to instruct their members to work for whichever anti-Tory was standing. Not every local association was willing to be guided by London; but enough of them were, so that in many constituencies up and down the country the Tory candidate was faced with one, and not two, anti-Tory opponents.

The result

It was fairly obvious that the Tories would lose the election whenever it was called. In the event the result was a fiasco for the Tories who won only 157 seats —even fewer than they had won in 1832. It seemed as if all Disraeli's work was undone. The Liberals, on the other hand, won 400 seats giving them an overall majority in the House of Commons. It seemed as if the splits of the last twenty

34 The House of Lords in session. For many people the House of Lords represented the last hope of stopping the rush towards socialism as preached by the radical Liberals led by Lloyd George

35 Winston Churchill returning to his hotel, acknowledging the cheers of the crowd after his election victory at Dundee, 1908. He had just become the President of the Board of Trade in succession to Lloyd George. Notice the placard about women's suffrage, and the woman on the left of the picture

years had been healed and that the freedom-loving British electorate had come to their senses again.

But the most significant feature of the new Commons was spotted by Balfour, the disconsolate leader of the Tory rump. He looked at the 53 Labour MPs and remarked: 'We have here to do with something bigger than a Liberal victory'. Who had elected these MPs but the very working classes on whom the Liberal Party had increasingly come to depend? Was there room in British politics for two parties of the Left? If not, would the Liberals move further to the Left and, by proposing radical policies, steal the Labour Party's clothes and the votes of their supporters? Or had the Liberal Party merely entered upon an Indian summer of success? Was the election result the beginnings of great things for the Liberals, or was it a swan song for an old party which had fulfilled its purposes by modernising the country under Gladstone, and was unable to come to terms with the twentieth century and its demands for social progress?

Balfour was a disappointed leader of a small Tory group but he had the satisfaction of appreciating the dilemma in which his Liberal opponents found themselves. To move further to the Left would frighten their older, faithful supporters even if it won the support of the lower classes; not to move to the Left would drive the working classes to support the Labour Party. Whichever happened Balfour and the Tories would live to fight for many another day—which was more than could be said of the Liberals.

6   1910: The Triumph of Democracy

In the period 1910–1914 many observers thought that the social structure of Britain was tearing itself apart. Everywhere one looked there was bitterness and strife; it seemed as if no part of the social fabric escaped as women, trade unions, the Irish (North and South), the socialists and even the House of Lords each contributed to the general picture of unrest.

Trade unions

Older people remembered the time when trade unions were small societies of skilled workmen; the Amalgamated Society of Engineers, with a membership of about 70,000 in 1880, was typical of these respectable unions. Most of their members voted Liberal, they accepted the Liberal idea of self-help, they did not believe in socialism (Chapter 5). They were proud to be free agents, bargaining, through their union, with the free employer; certainly they went on strike and sometimes there was violence as employers tried to break the strike; but in general the majority of people agreed with the Royal Commission of 1867 which had approved of trade unionism and recommended that laws be passed to strengthen the hands of union leaders.

By 1910 the union scene was quite different. In the 1880s there had come into being a number of unions for unskilled workers—in gasworks, match factories and, above all, for the dockers. These unions were from the start much larger than the older unions: the dockers' union had a membership of over 150,000. They were also much more militant—more willing to strike, less willing to negotiate with employers. Their leaders, Tillett, Mann and others, were socialists who believed that the government should actively help to make life better for the ordinary people.

One result of the emergence of these larger, more militant unions, was a change in the pattern of behaviour of the older unions. They too gradually became much larger, as small unions amalgamated to form larger ones and as they changed their rules to allow membership to unskilled workers. More significantly the larger, more militant unions began to think of themselves as national societies and whereas local strikes had once been called by Sheffield file grinders or Durham miners, after 1910 the country experienced the first of the national strikes by which the unions hoped to paralyse the country's trade.

Women

By 1910 women were much freer than they had been in the 1880s. In 1882 a married woman was allowed by law to own property—previously her property

36 The army and the police move in to break the national transport strike in 1912

became that of her husband. Inventions such as the telephone and the type-writer opened up new job opportunities for middle-class girls and an increasing number of them were going to work, to high schools and even to Universities. But the male-dominated Parliament refused to allow women the right to vote in Parliamentary elections. Some women had been campaigning for this right for many years; in 1903 Mrs Pankhurst founded a more militant organisation of women who, after 1910, used shock tactics to draw attention to their demands for equality.

Political unrest

Lloyd George was Chancellor of the Exchequer in the Liberal government when he spoke at Swansea in 1908 and tried to explain to his audience why Liberalism had to become more socialist than it had been under Gladstone:

> The new Liberalism ... devotes its endeavour ... to the removing of the immediate causes of discontent. It is true that men cannot live by bread alone. It is equally true that a man cannot live without bread ... It is a recognition of that elemental fact that has promoted legislation like the Old Age Pensions Act. It is but the beginning of things ... In so far as poverty is due to circumstances over which the man has no control, then the State should step in to the very utmost limit of its resources, and save the man from the physical and mental torture involved in extreme penury. ... We are confronted with the gigantic task of dealing with the rest—the sick, the infirm, the unemployed, the widows, and the orphans. No country can lay any real claim to civilisation that allows them to starve.

Lloyd George was aware of the emergence of the Labour Party as a radical rival to the Liberals (Chapter 5); he understood that the new party would grow stronger unless the Liberals changed their policies. But if the government was going to spend money on benefits for the old, the sick, the unemployed and widowed, then the level of taxation had to increase. In his 1909 budget Lloyd George proposed an increase in the level of death duties on estates over £5,000,

37 A sweat shop in the East End, 1904

a new super-tax payable in addition to income tax on incomes over £3,000 and a revolutionary tax on unearned increases in land values to be paid whenever a landowner sold any land for building or other purposes. Each of these new proposals was an attack on the wealth of the upper classes—most of whom were Tory—and, in the case of the aristocracy, many of whom had a seat in the House of Lords.

The House of Lords

In January 1906 the Tory leader Balfour, speaking at Manchester, said: 'It is the duty of everyone to ensure that the great Unionist party should still control whether in power or in opposition, the destinies of this great Empire'. Balfour and many Tories believed that the election result was a freak and that it was their duty—through the House of Lords—to preserve Britain from the follies of Liberal government.

The House of Lords had the power to throw out Bills put forward by the Commons. Between 1906 and 1909 the Lords either threw out or drastically altered many important Bills put forward by the Liberal Commons—on Education, the Welsh Church, Licensing Laws and others. One effect of this was to arouse the anger of Liberal politicians who could not get their programme through Parliament; another result was the disenchantment of the electorate with the

Liberals who had proposed so much and were, in fact, achieving so little. By-election results in this period, 1906–1909, showed a swing back to the Tories.

But most important of all, the Tories use of the Lords as a blocking mechanism raised the whole question: What sort of government does Britain have? Is it a democracy in which the will of the majority is reflected in the vote at a general election? Or is it some sort of oligarchy where a small group of Lords can determine what shall and what shall not be passed into law?

In 1909 Lloyd George's budget passed through the Commons only after a long, bitter debate. In December 1909 the Lords rejected this budget—something which had never happened before. Asquith advised the King to dissolve Parliament and to call a general election in January 1910. Lloyd George was the leading Liberal in this election which was yet another of the 'simple issue' elections. As Lloyd George said:

Should 500 men, ordinary men, over-ride the judgment of millions of people? They have slain the budget. In doing so they have killed the Bill which . . . had in it more promise of better things for the people of this country than most Bills that have been submitted to the House of Commons. It made provisions against the inevitable evils which befall such large masses of our poor population—their old age, infirmity, sickness and unemployment . . . And yet here you have an order of men blessed with every fortune . . . grudging a small pittance out of their super-abundance in order to protect those who have built up their wealth against the haunting terrors of misery and despair.

Well, now, we are on the eve of a general election, which will decide this great question. Who are the guardians of this mighty people? They are men who have neither the training, the qualifications, nor the experience which

38 Even in 1906 there was a great deal of heat in an election campaign. In this picture, the Prime Minister, Sir Henry Campbell-Bannerman, faces such a rowdy audience that he refused to continue, saying, 'I cannot go any further'

would fit them for such a gigantic task ... they are simply men whose sole qualification is that they are the first-born of persons who had just as little qualifications as they themselves.

Election, January 1910

The Liberals received an unexpected setback in this, the first of the 1910 elections. They won 272 seats while the Tories won 271; this meant that the Liberals had to depend on the support of the Labour Party with its 53 seats and, more significantly, on the support of Redmond and the Irish Nationalists with their 86 seats. Would the Irish give their support to a Liberal government which had made no attempt to introduce a Home Rule Bill while it had a massive majority?

Redmond agreed to support the Liberals, provided that they agreed to bring in a Home Rule Bill in the near future. Asquith agreed. But Redmond pointed out that the Lords had rejected a Home Rule Bill in 1893. Would they do the same to the next Liberal Home Rule Bill? Was there not a case for so altering the power of the Lords that they could not thwart the will of the Commons?

Lloyd George and the radical Liberals agreed with this; they wanted their revenge on the Lords for having obstructed so much of their business between 1906 and 1909, and, in particular, for having rejected the 1909 budget.

The Parliament Bill

While the Lords now passed the budget (1910) the Liberals put forward a Bill which provided that the Lords was to lose its power to amend or reject any Money Bill (such as a budget); that any Bill passed by the Commons in three successive sessions should become law even if rejected three times by the Lords, and that general elections should be held every five years instead of every seven. This Bill, of course, the Lords rejected in 1910.

A series of conferences between Party leaders was called by King Edward VII, whose death in 1910 accentuated the air of constitutional crisis. His son, King George V, agreed with Asquith's proposals that if the Parliament Bill was put before the people at another election he should create all the new peers needed to out-number the opposition. A list of about 300 names was prepared.

39 Liberals at their headquarters, the National Liberal Club, London, rejoicing at the news of the defeat of the Conservative leader, Balfour, at Manchester. Free Trade and radicalism seemed to be victorious

40 *The Trojan Horse.* Lord Halsbury is pulling the Horse with its 500 Peers, while Lord Lansdowne is trying to persuade the die-hard opponents of Liberalism to give in, rather than have another 500 Liberal Peers

Election, December 1910

This second election had a similar result to the first; the Liberals had a majority of one over the Tories and were virtually prisoners of the Irish. The Parliament Bill was put forward again and after a bitter debate in the Lords, was finally approved. The constitutional crisis, at least, was over. Or was it?

Future problems

One of the lesser by-products of the new Parliament Act, 1911 was the payment of a salary of £400 a year to MPs. This was of immediate benefit to the infant Labour Party, whose MPs had been paid out of trade union funds. The chances of a working man becoming an MP were increased by this measure.

One of the more important by-products of the Act and the crisis surrounding it was that the Liberals brought in an Irish Home Rule Bill in 1912. Under the terms of the 1911 Act the Lords could reject this in two sessions (1912 and 1913) but when the Bill was put forward again in 1914 the Lords knew that they had no power to change the course of history. The Irish were to get Home Rule in 1914, come what may.

To the Tories who owned land in Ireland and to the Irish Protestants it was

61

41 Sir Edward Carson (centre, without a hat) leaving the Great Ulster Rally in Hyde Park in April 1914. Upper- and middle-class Tory Protestants were preparing for civil war against Home Rule and the Liberal government

a bitter blow; from being part of the Protestant majority in the United Kingdom they would become part of the minority in Catholic Ireland. Home Rule would indeed be Rome Rule.

Civil War?

In particular this was a bitter blow to the Protestants of the four counties surrounding Belfast, where the Protestants were in a majority of the population. Was Ulster to be ruled from Dublin? Not if the Tories and the Protestants could help it. Bonar Law had become the Party leader when Balfour retired. Speaking at a monster rally at the Duke of Marlborough's Palace at Blenheim in 1912, he said: 'if an attempt was made . . . as part of a corrupt Parliamentary bargain, to deprive these men of their birthright, they would be justified in resisting by all means in their power, including force.'

In Ulster itself the Tory leaders, Carson, Craig and Smith, organised the signing of the Belfast Covenant, which read:

Being convinced in our consciences that Home Rule would be disastrous to the material well-being of Ulster as well as the whole of Ireland, subversive of our civil and religious freedom, destructive of our citizenship, and perilous to the unity of the Empire, we, whose names are underwritten, men of Ulster, loyal subjects of His Gracious Majesty . . . humbly relying on the God whom our fathers in days of stress and trial confidently trusted, do hereby pledge ourselves in solemn Covenant throughout this our time of threatened calamity to stand by one another in defending for ourselves and our children our cherished possession of equal citizenship in the United Kingdom, and in using all means which may be found necessary to defeat the present conspiracy to set up a Home Rule Parliament in Ireland. And in the event of such a Parliament being forced upon us we further solemnly and mutually pledge ourselves to refuse to recognize its authority. In sure confidence that God will defend the right we hereto subscribe our names. God Save the King.

The Tories, once the constitutional party, now began to plan for a civil war in which the Protestants of Ulster were to fight the British government. Guns were bought in Germany and brought to Belfast; a Volunteer Army was formed, drilled by British officers; stately homes in England were fitted up as field hospitals to which the Protestant wounded would be brought.

An end to social unrest

Women, the working class, the Lords, the Protestants of Ulster and the Tories of England were all sources of unrest. But when Germany invaded Belgium in August 1914 and the Liberal government declared war, these troubles were put aside. The militant women changed their slogan to 'We demand the right to serve'; Redmond and the Nationalists agreed to postpone the Irish Home Rule Bill until the Germans had been defeated; trade unions agreed to alter their rules to allow unskilled workers to do work previously done only by skilled men. In the face of the war crisis the country returned to the semblance of unity. We who have lived through the Ulster crisis of the 1970s know that the unity was, for some at least, only an appearance and not a reality.

42 A recruiting poster produced in 1914 when trade unionists, Irish nationalists, suffragettes and Tory rebels forgot the past—for a time

THERE'S ROOM FOR YOU

ENLIST TO-DAY

7 1923: The People into Limited Power

Lloyd George, the war-winner

Lloyd George had first become a household name as a 'Little Englander' opposed to Chamberlain and the Boer War (Chapter 5). He had become a leading force in the Liberal Party as the leading advocate of the 'New Liberalism' with its emphasis on social welfare (Chapter 6). When the First World War broke out in 1914 he was as wholehearted in waging war as once he had been in opposing Chamberlain in 1900 or the Lords in 1909–1911.

By 1916 the War was going badly; in spite of continued promises from politicians and generals that 'it will all be over by Christmas' the terrible slaughter went on. Many people believed that one reason for Britain's lack of success was that the Prime Minister, Asquith, was not as wholeheartedly in favour of war as he ought to have been. There was no sense of urgency; industrialists were allowed to produce what they wanted—if the government wouldn't pay high prices for munitions, the factories didn't produce them; if sufficient men wouldn't volunteer for the services, the government wouldn't compel them to enlist. The Liberal idea of freedom came into conflict with the urgent necessity of fully mobilising the country's resources.

During the constitutional crisis over the budget in 1910, Lloyd George had spoken to the leaders of the Tory Party, suggesting a Coalition government—of Liberals and Tories—as one way of overcoming the crisis. In 1916 the Tories attacked Asquith's ability as war-leader and, led by Bonar Law and Balfour, they agreed to serve as members of a Coalition government under Lloyd George. This angered those Liberals who supported Asquith and the split in the Liberal Party, evident in the 1900s (Chapter 5), was re-opened.

43 Lloyd George at Victoria Station with King George V and the Prince of Wales, after his return from the Versailles Conference, June 1919

Lloyd George's government included the leaders of the Tory Party—Chamberlain, Bonar Law, Balfour, Carson, Smith—as well as Labour leaders Arthur Henderson and J. R. Clynes. Lord Beaverbrook, remembering that government, wrote: 'Many will say that Lloyd George's greatest days ... were in times of peace when he put upon the Statute Book more social legislation than any single statesman in our history; but I do not hold that view. To me his greatest hour came as late as the Spring of 1918, when ... our troops were in retreat, the Russian Armies were out of the war, and the American Armies had not yet come in ... It was then his leadership showed itself supreme, his courage untarnished. No other moment in Britain's recurring story of escape from disaster can surpass it.'

The 1918 election

Once the war was over, Lloyd George led his Coalition friends into a general election. Only the Labour Party and the Asquithian Liberals offered candidates to oppose the Coalition candidates, each of whom received a letter of support from Lloyd George. Leo Amery was a candidate; he remembered: 'The manifesto issued by Lloyd George and Bonar Law was a broad progressive document. It pledged itself to dealing with Ireland ... India ... the House of Lords ... the protection of industry ... and to social reform. The high opening note of the campaign was not long sustained. [The election] appealed to the demagogic side of Lloyd George's nature, and made him indulge in fantastic promises about trying the Kaiser and demanding from Germany the whole cost of the war. Lloyd George swept the board. Barely a couple of dozen Asquithian Liberals survived the catastrophe, and that without their leader.'

Another writer commented: 'The general election of 1918 involved a vulgarisation of British public life. With the enlarged electorate, [and with the women], there were growing numbers of the electors whose politics were not based on well-defined doctrines. ... the ready prey of the vulgarisers in political journalism and, finally, in political leadership ... such slogans as "Hang the Kaiser", or "Squeeze the lemon until the pips squeak" gave them convenient matter for private oratory. [In this] Lloyd George played his part. Thus he collected his Parliament of what Mr Baldwin called "hard-faced men who look as if they have done very well out of the war".'

Lloyd George out of office

By 1922 the war hero had become the villain of the piece—or peace. As Lord Beaverbrook recalled:

The war was over. Lloyd George was now the most powerful man in Europe. His fame would endure for ever ... He had beaten his German enemies, he had scattered and destroyed his British enemies at the polls ... But in politics nothing is permanent. So it was with the reputation of Lloyd George ... It is hard to explain to a new generation the full measure of dislike, distrust, even loathing, with which the public came to regard his government.

All the while unemployment was widespread throughout the land. These domestic miseries sharpened the impatience with which the public regarded Lloyd George's busy and impulsive foreign policy . . . But the immediate cause of his fall may have been his arrogance. A Prime Minister without a party cannot dispense with the trust . . . of his supporters in the House of Commons. At the very height of his popularity he became impatient, critical and dictatorial in manner . . . his strength depended on his personal ascendancy with the public; and upon the Conservative political machine which was only used effectively for Lloyd George's benefit so long as Bonar Law was its custodian.

Some Tories, much the largest single group within the Coalition Party, decided to rid themselves of this dictator. In 1922 those who still wanted to support Lloyd George called a meeting at the Carlton Club, to whip up support from their fellow-Tories. Chamberlain, Curzon, Smith—the leading lights of the Party—spoke in favour of continuing their support of Lloyd George. Stanley Baldwin, then only the Financial Secretary of the Treasury and not at all well known to the public, spoke against this motion. The respected leader, Bonar Law, let it be known that he was prepared to lead the Party into a general election, and to the surprise of the leading Tories, the Coalition came to an end.

The unknown Prime Minister

Bonar Law called for a general election in 1922 and the Tories won 354 seats—a majority of 77 over all other parties combined. The Labour Party, led by

44 Stanley Baldwin (second from left, seated) having defeated Lloyd George in 1922, with Imperial Prime Ministers at the Imperial Conference 1923. Smuts, Britain's opponent in the Boer War, is sitting on the extreme right of the picture

MacDonald, won 142 seats and so became the official opposition, a major step forward in the history of this still-new party. The Liberals were split— Asquith's followers won 65 seats and Lloyd George's Liberal supporters won 52.

But Bonar Law was a sick man and in May 1923 he retired. The leading Tories—Chamberlain and others—had refused to serve under Bonar Law; his successor had to be one of the 'second eleven' who had formed the Cabinet. King George v was advised by Balfour, Bonar Law and others, to send for Stanley Baldwin, who became Prime Minister.

In a speech he made at this time, Baldwin said: 'To me, at least, this unemployment problem is the most critical problem of our country . . . And I have come to the conclusion myself that the only way of fighting this subject is by protecting the home market.' The promises of 'making a country fit for heroes to live in' looked very hollow to the hundreds of thousands of men who could not find work. Baldwin did not know it, of course, but this was the beginning of that economic depression which led to an average unemployment figure of about 2 million a year right up to 1939. The Tariff Reformers now reopened their case first presented in 1903 (Chapter 5). They argued that if only Britain abandoned Free Trade, and imposed tariffs on foreign goods employment prospects would improve.

Baldwin was unwilling to adopt this policy without first getting the approval of the electorate, so in 1923 he called an election in which he proposed a policy of Protection. The Liberals reunited in an uneasy alliance to fight this ancient enemy of Tariff Reform: the combined Asquithians and Lloyd Georgites won 157 seats—a great improvement on their performance in 1922. The Tories won 258 seats showing that Tariff Reform was obviously not a popular policy. The most significant feature of the election result was that the Labour Party won 192 seats.

Baldwin appreciated that he could not form a government to implement a policy of Tariff Reform which the country had rejected. He could have formed a government with support from the Liberals and tried to solve the country's economic problems in some other way. But Baldwin had a great dislike and distrust of Lloyd George whom he suspected of plotting with Chamberlain and other Tories to form a Lloyd George Coalition. As one Conservative wrote: 'The one dominant motive . . . with him was fear of Lloyd George and his influence. It was fear of L.G.'s influence, combined with Winston's, over Austen and F.E. that led to the amazing offer of the Exchequer to Winston. Later on it was largely to keep out Winston and Lloyd George that he consented to the no less disastrous coalition with Ramsay MacDonald.'

Labour in power
Baldwin advised King George v to send for the leader of the next largest Party in the Commons and ask him to try to form a government. To some, Tory and Liberal, this was a betrayal of all that was good and right—to admit the Bolshevik Labourites to office. But Baldwin realised that if he tried to deprive Labour of

their rightful claim (to try to form a government) there might be trouble in the country—either immediately or in the future. If working men believed that their representatives were being cheated out of office by an unholy alliance of Tories and Liberals, then they might decide to take more violent action in support of their demands for a better life.

Baldwin also realised that a Labour government taking office in 1923 would not be able to do anything very rash—since it did not have a majority in the House of Commons. This would give the Labour leaders a chance to get into office, learn the problems of running Ministries, of framing budgets, of negotiating with foreign governments—all in a sort of 'safety net' of an anti-Labour majority in the House of Commons.

Another Tory leader, Balfour, had spotted the importance of the 1906 election in which 53 Labour MPs entered the Commons. Baldwin was equally perceptive; he realised that at some stage in the future the Labour Party might win a commanding majority in the Commons. Since this was so it was a good thing to let the leaders of this Labour Party practise the art of government in a situation where they could be controlled.

And so in January 1924 MacDonald presented his government to the King, who wrote in his diary: 'What would grandmamma have thought?' A Labour Minister wrote of their first interview with the King, 'As we stood waiting for His Majesty, amid the gold and crimson of the Palace, I could not help marvelling at the strange turn of Fortune's wheel which had brought MacDonald the starveling clerk, Thomas the engine-driver, Henderson the foundry labourer and Clynes the mill-hand to this pinnacle'.

A new epoch had begun in British politics. The people's party which had got its first representative into Parliament in 1893 had, by 1923, replaced the Liberal

45 Ramsay MacDonald at the Labour Party Victory Demonstration, 1924. On his left is Margaret Bondfield, the first woman member of the Cabinet, J. H. Thomas, General Secretary of the National Union of Railwaymen and Robert Smillie, of the Miners' Federation, and architect of the Triple Alliance which led to the General Strike, 1926

46 A former chairman of the TUC, Harry Gosling, supervising the pasting up of election posters, February 1923. Many right-wing politicians tried to show that the mild-mannered Gosling and his companions were attempting to lead a Bolshevik revolution

Party as the natural opposition to the Tories, and in 1924 formed the first Labour government. The experiment was short-lived. In 1924 MacDonald called another election—the third in three years, and Baldwin won a resounding success, as his biographer recalls:

> It became the fashion in Socialist circles to maintain that the election of 1924 was won by a trick . . . In truth, the Red Letter did little more than add a certain excitement to what both parties knew to be a foregone conclusion. Twelve months had been enough to show the electorate . . . that the Socialists were no more competent to deal with the malady of unemployment than their opponents; that a Socialist victory would mean another short Parliament and another general election at no distant date. Baldwin offered stability, the very thing which he seemed to embody in face, in build, in the accent of his voice. And to the new electorate personality counted far more than policy. . . . No one knew what a MacDonald government would do or not do next. [The one thing certain] was that powerful elements of the Left had transferred their allegiance to a foreign power, which was working, not silently and secretly but loudly and ostentatiously for the subversion of English institutions.

Many Labour supporters were disappointed and some decided that industrial action was a quicker way of getting a 'new society'; they supported the campaign for a general strike which took place in 1926—and which proved to the majority of the Labour Party supporters that the slow process of political change was a better weapon than the clumsy and unsuccessful weapon of the strike.

Many Liberal supporters were also disillusioned as the results of the 1924 election show. From now on the two-Party system which prevails in British politics worked to squeeze the Liberals between the radical Labour Party and the conserving Tories; there was little room left for the Liberals, whose few successes were gained on the Celtic fringes of West Wales and North Scotland.

8 1945: 'A Most Surprising Result'

On 8 May 1945 the Germans signed a general armistice and unconditionally surrendered to the forces of the USA, Britain and France. The most destructive war in the world's history was almost over—although Japan had still to be defeated and the Far East reconquered for the various colonial powers—Holland, France and Britain.

Since 10 May 1940, almost exactly five years to the day of surrender, Winston Churchill had been Prime Minister and had invited Labour and Liberal leaders to sit in his Cabinet. This Coalition government had not only waged a successful war against Hitler and Japan, it had also produced a series of blueprints or signposts for that 'better Britain' which Lloyd George had promised in 1918 (Chapter 7), but had failed to deliver. This Coalition government had appointed the Beveridge Committee, a Committee on the coal industry, a population Commission; it had produced a White Paper on Full Employment, had established the Ministry of National Insurance and had passed the 1944 Education Act along with the Family Allowance Act, 1945.

If the war was most destructive it had also been, in another sense, the most constructive one that the world had ever seen. Never had a nation at war so prepared itself for the transition to peace; never had a nation produced such a set of plans for transforming the whole economic and social fabric of its life. Post-war Britain, obviously, was going to be a much different place from the depressed Britain of the 1930s.

Election day

Churchill would have preferred not to hold an election until the war with Japan was over. He would also have preferred to take his Coalition government with him into the election, as his hero, Lloyd George, had done in 1918. Churchill had never been a great Party politician and he did not think that the immediate post-war years were ones in which Britain could afford the luxury of party squabbles.

The leading members of the Labour Party who sat with him in the government were inclined to agree; but the Labour backbenchers and the Labour rank and file made it clear to their leaders that the Labour Party should withdraw from the Coalition and fight an election as soon as was possible. Some of these, at any rate, had remembered the fate of the 1918 Coalition which had become a Tory government in 1922 (Chapter 7).

On 15 June, Parliament was dissolved and Polling Day was fixed for July 5. Because of the armed forces scattered throughout the world it would take some

47 On 10 May 1945, Field-Marshal Montgomery (in beret) visited the Russian Marshal Rokossovsky at his headquarters. Exactly five years before this Churchill had become Prime Minister

time for votes to be counted and recorded and 26 July was fixed as the day on which the election result would be declared.

Churchill and the election

Churchill had never been a strong Party man; he had started out in life as a Tory, the son of a former Tory Chancellor of the Exchequer: he had left the Tories during the controversy over Tariff Reform (Chapter 5) and became a Liberal Minister in 1906. He had supported Lloyd George's Coalition government after 1916: in 1922 he had been opposed to the Carlton Club decision (Chapter 7) but had been invited to join the Baldwin Cabinet in 1924 when he was surprisingly appointed Chancellor of the Exchequer. He up-valued the pound, which had been worth \$4.20, to \$4.80. This led to a further fall in the level of British exports, which became dearer than goods sold by foreign competitors. He had quarrelled with Baldwin over his plans for eventual Home Rule for India and he rashly supported Edward VIII during the Abdication Crisis in 1936. Although he was right in his warnings about the dangers from Germany, few people believed him because he had been proved so hopelessly wrong about other things.

After 1940 he became a national hero whose speeches reflected the determination of the British people not to surrender to Germany. Once the election campaign got under way in 1945 his popularity was shown by the tremendous crowds who attended his meetings and cheered him on his way. He and his advisers must have thought that the British people were bound to 'Vote Churchill,

48 The destructive war: a London bus in a bomb crater

49 London mothers with their 'under fives' boarding the Evacuation Special. This evacuation was just one of the many ways in which social classes mixed in war time Britain as they had never done before

Vote Tory' in the election which would be as great a victory for this war hero as 1918 had been for Lloyd George.

The Labour Party

Few of the leading figures in the Labour Party disagreed with this view; they, too, expected a Churchill victory. Attlee had been Deputy Prime Minister; Morrison, Home Secretary; Bevin, Minister of Labour, and other Labour politicians had held senior posts in the government. But they believed that the British people would see this as Churchill's Government, Churchill's War and Churchill's Peace.

Some Labour leaders, notably Aneurin Bevan, argued that the Party would win the election. They pointed out that the war had been a constructive one which had raised people's expectations of a better life after that war. Beveridge's Report had been a popular best-seller; J. B. Priestley's broadcasts, with their emphasis on the unfairness of life in the 1930s had attracted record audiences; throughout the world the Service chiefs had organised an Education Service where young teachers helped to lead discussions on a vast range of subjects— including Britain past, present and future. One of his Air Force chiefs, Bomber Harris, warned Churchill that about 80 per cent of the Service vote would be anti-Tory. Churchill refused to believe him. As Herbert Morrison wrote later:

> Political myopia [short-sightedness] is the only diagnosis that can be given for the Tories' utter ignorance of the new outlook of the people. Counting on winning solely through the nation's admiration for its war leader the Tories offered nothing but idol worship and a programme of negation, plus some absurd scares.
>
> One of the most important features of the 1945 election was the proxy vote … The *Daily Mirror* published a letter (from a woman reader) which said 'I shall vote for him,' referring to the hopes of her soldier husband for a better Britain, and so began a campaign built round the slogan 'Vote for Him'. It … undoubtedly influenced large numbers of women, who had hitherto imagined that politics were of no importance to them, to think about them and to discuss the subject in their letters to their husbands.

The people

The war had thrown together people of all classes; children from the overcrowded cities had been evacuated to the middle-class suburbs and country towns; men from all backgrounds were conscripted and served together in the various Services; older men served in war-time organisations such as ARP and the Home Guard, and shared duties like fire-watching; women mixed together as members of the Forces or as firewatchers, ambulance drivers. Never had the social classes been so thoroughly shaken up.

This mixing of the classes had at least two major effects. The better-off classes

50 Attlee at Labour's celebration meeting in London in July 1945. Seated on his right is Herbert Morrison; to the left of the table is Ernest Bevin. The British people refused to believe that these meant to introduce a Gestapo-like system of control

saw, at first hand, the effects of poverty; into their suburban homes they took the underfed, badly-clothed and often ill-mannered children of London and other major cities. Men and women who had been prepared to say: 'It's their own fault' when they read about unemployment, poverty, overcrowding or the like, found themselves unable to say this when they met the victims for the first time. This wartime experience caused many of the better-off to join with the less well-off in pressing for a better Britain after 1945.

The less well-off, on the other hand, had their first experience of living with the better-educated and better-off: 'You worked alongside people you had hardly ever spoken to before, doctors, lawyers, civil servants. Sometimes there would be arguments about politics, music and religion. You would realise how lucky people were if they had been educated, and make up your mind to see that your children had a decent education'.

Christopher Hollis was a Tory MP after 1945 and he wrote: 'However we may have voted in 1945, none of us looking back can deny that there was at that time a general feeling of disgust in the nation, just or unjust, with the past'.

The campaign

As Morrison pointed out, the Tory campaign was a negative one based almost entirely on support for Churchill. Neither he nor his Party managers were whole-hearted in their support of the policies that had been proposed by Beveridge and by other Commissions. Many of the electorate believed that a vote for Churchill might indeed be a vote for a return to yesterday. As Beveridge himself pointed out: 'At the end of the First War we thought of going back to the good old times. During the Second War we realised that we must go forward and not back, because the times between the wars were not good ... The view of Conservative organisers is that it is easier for voters to be persuaded to vote against something than to be persuaded to vote for anything'. Clearly, the people

51 Major Denis Healey speaking at the Labour Party Conference, June 1945. Healey symbolised the millions of servicemen who were to vote for the Labour Party at the election which this Conference demanded

of the country were determined to vote against the Conservatives on this occasion.

In his first broadcast to the nation Churchill warned them that 'There can be no doubt that Socialism is inseparably interwoven with totalitarianism and the abject worship of the State . . . Socialism is in its essence an attack not only on British enterprise, but upon the right of an ordinary man or woman to breathe freely without having a harsh, clumsy, tyrannical hand clapped across their mouth and nostrils. A free Parliament is odious to the Socialist doctrinaire'.

To most people this seemed a ridiculous accusation to make about mild-mannered Mr Attlee and his other colleagues who, until a few weeks previously, had been members of Churchill's own Cabinet. Attlee took advantage of Churchill's error and thanked him for 'warning the electors to understand how great was the difference between Winston Churchill, the great leader in war of a united nation, and Mr Churchill, the party leader of the Conservatives . . . I thank him for having disillusioned them so thoroughly. The voice we heard last night was that of Mr Churchill, but the mind was that of Lord Beaverbrook'. However, throughout the rest of the campaign Churchill continued to attract the crowds and continued to believe that he had won.

The result

On 26 July the results were declared and the Labour Party, with 393 seats to 189 for the Tories, had a bigger majority than any party had ever had in modern times—much larger than that of the Liberals in 1906 (Chapter 5). Attlee recalled later that King George v had been almost speechless when the Labour leader went to the Palace to receive the commission to form a government; Attlee himself was more than a little surprised. So, too, were many of the electorate; one woman diner at Claridge's Hotel, London, shrieked: 'They've elected a Labour government; the country will never stand for it'—indicating both surprise and a

Daily Mail

FOR KING AND EMPIRE

NO. 15,358   ONE PENNY ★ ★ FRIDAY, JULY 27, 1945

Labour Government, 416: Opposition, 211—Majority, 205

CHURCHILL RESIGNS: ATTLEE FORMING HIS CABINET

New Premier may go back to 'Big 3' alone

By WILSON BROADBENT, *Political Correspondent*

MR. WINSTON CHURCHILL drove to Buckingham Palace early yesterday evening, very soon after Labour's mounting victories at the polls had reached their sensational climax. Formally tendering his resignation as Prime Minister, he advised the King to send for Mr. Attlee.

As Leader of the Labour Party, Mr. Attlee will to-day consult his colleagues about the immediate formation of the new Government as provided by the terms of the Labour Party's constitution.

Before midday he is expected to be in a position to inform the King of his plans. Although it is possible for the Labour Executive to insist on some other person assuming the office of Prime Minister—there were rumours last night that discussions on this point had started—the general belief is that Mr. Attlee will be Mr. Churchill's successor.

In these matters, if in little else, the Labour Party can be described as very "conservative." Last night Mr. Attlee stated : "I expect to form a new Government at once, and then I shall go back to Potsdam."

While the defeat of the Churchill Government extends in drama the rout of the Labour Party in 1931, there is a combination which is without precedent in modern times.

The new Prime Minister leaves to take his place without delay all the vital international involvement at Potsdam and home questions of a Government as well.

Something good every day in your Daily Mail

TODAY we publish the first eight-page *Daily Mail* since June 29, 1940. It is for one day only, but it foreshadows a permanently bigger *Daily Mail*.

THE NEW CABINET

Morrison 'tipped' as Chancellor

By Daily Mail Political Correspondent

MR. HERBERT MORRISON, former Home Secretary, who organised Labour's successful election campaign, was last night forecast as Britain's new Chancellor of the Exchequer.

Still smiling

Churchill gives thanks to people

Mr. Churchill issued the following statement from No. 10, Downing-street, last night :

"THE decision of the British people has been recorded in the votes counted to-day. I have, therefore, laid down the charge which was placed upon me in darker times.

"I regret that I have not been permitted to finish the work against Japan. For this, however, all plans and preparations have been made, and the results may come much quicker than we have hitherto been entitled to expect.

"Immense responsibilities abroad and at home fall upon the new Government, and we must all hope that they will be successful in bearing them.

"It only remains for me to express to the British people, for whom I have acted in these perilous years, my profound gratitude for the unflinching, unswerving support which they have given me during my task, and for the many expressions of kindness which they have shown towards their servant."

PM HINTS AT QUICK PEACE

3 Powers send an ultimatum to Japan

SURRENDER—OR RUIN

From EDWIN TETLOW, Daily Mail Special Correspondent

BRITAIN, the United States, and China have sent a joint ultimatum to Japan warning her to get out of the war on Allied terms now or be "completely destroyed by the prodigious forces now poised to strike the final blows."

The proclamation, signed by Mr. Churchill and President Truman while they were in Potsdam, and approved by Marshal Chiang Kai-shek by radio, sets out terms which amount to unconditional surrender.

Saddest day and last

By Daily Mail Political Correspondent

£22,000 was lost by 148

Forfeited deposits

LASKI THANKS CHURCHILL

'Great services'

On other pages

The riddle of the last result

Go-slow 'wins'

By Daily Mail Reporter

STATE OF PARTIES

STATE of the parties, with the exception of 12 University results to be announced later, and Central Hull, where a by-election has to be fought.

For New Govt.

		Agst. New Govt.
Labour	390	Conservative	165
Liberal	10	National	3
		Nat. Liberal	14
Communist	2	Ind. Liberal	
		Nat. Labour	
	416		211

Gains and Losses

	Gain	Loss		Gain	Loss
Labour			Conservative		
Liberal			National		
Independent			Lib. National		
Communist					
For New Govt.			Agst New Govt.		

Aggregate Vote

Labour	11,981,401
Liberal	2,221,145
Conservative	9,658,412
National	137,719

Total 14,874,051

BACK PAGE—Col. SIX

BACK PAGE—Col. THREE

lack of understanding of 'they' and of 'the country'. Churchill recalled later that he was very gloomy. His wife tried to cheer him up with the view that perhaps God intended the result to be a lesson for the war-hero, perhaps God had a hidden plan in this let-down. 'Well' growled Churchill, 'He has kept it well hidden from me'.

Effects

For the first time in its history the Labour Party was really in power; unlike the MacDonald governments of the 1920s, Attlee had a majority in the Commons. Unlike MacDonald, Attlee controlled a team of Ministers many of whom had experience in government gained during the war.

Above all, the Attlee government came into power with the support of a majority which expected the creation of a better Britain. By 1947 this seemed to have been accomplished as one after another of the Acts creating the modern Welfare State rolled out. The Tories realised the extent of the change that had taken place within such a short time. Addressing the Young Conservative Annual Conference in 1949, Sir (later, Lord) Robert Boothby said that the country had gone through 'the greatest social revolution in its history', while Mr Butler, the architect of the 1944 Education Act, said: 'I think we should take pride that the British race has been able, shortly after the terrible period (1939–1945) through which we have passed together, to show the world that we are able to produce a social insurance scheme of this character'.

9   1959: 'They Have Never Had it so Good' and the Tories Win Again

Tory freedom

When the Tories were returned to power in 1951, Mr Churchill led a strong government which included Anthony Eden as Deputy Prime Minister and R. A. Butler as Chancellor of the Exchequer. Butler's policies were aimed at maintaining the 'social revolution' while, at the same time, lowering the level of taxation; the one was designed to maintain Tory popularity with those who had gained from the social changes, while the other was designed to win popularity from the better-off who paid most taxes.

Butler, like Labour Chancellors before him, found that running the economy was a tricky business. As soon as business picked up, so did the level of imports and unless this was matched by increases in exports the country experienced a balance of payments crisis. Butler, like Labour Chancellors before him, used a variety of weapons to try to solve this problem; the Bank rate was increased, credit squeeze was introduced and hire purchase transactions were rigidly controlled. All these were designed to make it more difficult for people at home to buy goods, so forcing manufacturers to export their goods.

Credit squeezes and restrictions are never popular with the voters—as the Labour government discovered in the 1960s. More particularly these measures did not fit in with the slogan 'Set the People Free', which won the Tories the 1951 election.

Anthony Eden became Prime Minister in 1955 when Churchill retired. He warned Butler that he would like to have an election in May 1955 and the April budget removed some of the restrictions on home consumption, lowered taxation and indicated that under the Tories the economy could be controlled quickly and successfully. All was set for a further period of freedom and expansion. In May the Eden government won 345 seats to the Labour Party's 277.

Economic crisis

But all was not well. As Eden recalls in his *Memoirs*: 'A few weeks after the election our economy began to feel twinges in the balance of payments. Increases in wages were influencing prices. By the end of August our gold and dollar reserves were falling. The country was attempting to do too much with the limited resources. To be effective our action against inflation had to curb both government and private spending. The Chancellor presented his proposals to the Commons in a budget on 26 October. It had a rough reception from the Opposition.' No surprising—since it was only a few months since the Tory election manifesto had stressed the strength of the economy indicated by the tax cuts in the April budget.

Suez, 1956

This was a bad beginning for the Eden government, but worse was to follow. On 19 July 1956 the Egyptian government, led by Colonel Nasser, learned that both the USA and British governments had withdrawn their previous offers of help to Egypt in building the Aswan High Dam—a project (now completed) which allows the Egyptians to provide electricity for many millions of its people and also permits controlled irrigation of the fertile Nile area, thus increasing food and cotton production and raising the Egyptian standard of living.

Nasser resented this abrupt withdrawal of aid and on 26 July 1956—in a speech to a cheering crowd—he announced that the Egyptian government would nationalise the Suez Canal and would use the revenue from the Canal to finance the building of the Dam. For several months various attempts were made by Commonwealth Prime Ministers and by UNO officials to work out a settlement

53 The President of the Glasgow University Labour Club being howled down by students who disagree with his speech against the Eden government's Suez policy

which would satisfy the Egyptians and the previous British and French shareholders in the Canal Company. None of the negotiations seemed likely to end Egyptian control of the Canal: in spite of forebodings from British and French officials, the Canal still operated.

Eden said: 'The unilateral decision of the Egyptian Government to expropriate the Suez Canal Company, without notice and in breach of the Concession agreements, affects the rights and interests of many nations. Her Majesty's Government are consulting other governments immediately concerned with regard to the serious situation thus created'.

There are conflicting accounts of what happened in the summer of 1956. What seems certain is that in October 1956 leaders of the British, French and Israeli governments met at Sèvres, in France, and agreed to invade Egypt. On 29 October 1956, Israel attacked; in six days they had defeated the Egyptian army and reached the Gulf of Akaba. On 30 October, British and French troops landed at Port Said after an air and sea bombardment.

The Labour Opposition declared: 'British people are profoundly shocked and ashamed that British aircraft should be bombing Egypt, not in self-defence, not in collective defence, but in clear defiance of the United Nations Charter', to which Eden replied: 'This is essentially a police operation. We do not intend to stay one moment more than is necessary . . . The whole purpose of the Anglo-French interventions is to stop hostilities . . . and to safeguard traffic through the Canal'.

The Russians threatened to declare war if Britain did not evacuate Egyptian territory and the USA, formerly and later our friend, demanded our withdrawal. At the United Nations the British nation was condemned almost unanimously. After a week's occupation British forces withdrew.

For a time the country was divided as it had not been since the 1930s. In clubs, pubs, offices, schools, factories and bus queues the rights and wrongs of the Suez adventure were discussed, often violently. Mass demonstrations were organised against Eden and the war, and the Tory Party's popularity sank further. One group opposed the government for having declared war, another element opposed the government for not having had the courage to stand up to Russia and America, and go ahead with its avowed policy of overthrowing Nasser and reclaiming the Canal. As in the crisis of 1828–1830 over Catholic Emancipation, a Tory government found itself under attack from two sides.

Colonial problems
The Macmillan government also had to contend with a number of problems resulting from the break up of the British Empire. In 1952 the Mau Mau uprising in Kenya had led to the declaration of a state of emergency and the sending of British troops to put down this barbaric attempt by black Africans to end the era of white domination. In 1959 the newspapers began to print reports of torture and cruelty being practised against Mau Mau prisoners at the Hola detention

camp in Kenya. At first the government denied that this could be the case; closer examination by an independent, government-appointed commission revealed that indeed there had been a series of outrages committed against black prisoners by white troops and police. The government was condemned by the Opposition and by liberal opinion generally for its support of the policy which had led to Hola.

In 1957 Ghana, formerly the Gold Coast, became the first independent Black African country. This stimulated the independence movements in other colonial territories. When Belgium hurriedly granted independence to her former colony in the Congo, black African leaders in Nyasaland (now Malawi) and Northern Rhodesia (now Zambia) began to ask that they too should be given their freedom. In Nyasaland there was the declaration of a state of emergency and British troops were sent to quell an uprising, said by the British government and the white rulers of the then Central African Federation, to be the work of a handful of trouble-makers. Macmillan appointed Judge Devlin to head a Commission to look into the causes of this uprising. The commission was condemned by the Opposition because Devlin's three colleagues were well-known Conservatives. In July 1959 the Commission reported, condemning the white domination of Central Africa, rejecting the idea that only a handful of trouble-makers supported the demand for independence. Once again government policy was in shreds. Was the Macmillan government to give independence to the rebellious blacks—and so lose the support of the imperially-minded British electorate, or was it to deny this demand for freedom, send in British troops to maintain white domination—and so lose the support of the more liberally-minded?

The Labour Opposition
A general election would have to be held in 1960 at the latest. No Prime Minister likes to call the election at the latest possible date; he never knows what crisis might blow up as that fateful last minute approaches; he prefers to call the election earlier rather than later, at whatever time he judges to be most favourable for his Party. So it seemed highly likely that Macmillan would call an election sometime in 1959.

Hugh Gaitskell led a confident Labour Opposition. They hoped they would

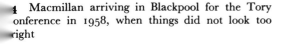

4 Macmillan arriving in Blackpool for the Tory Conference in 1958, when things did not look too bright

benefit from the unpopularity of a government which had hoodwinked the electorate with its promises of freedom in 1955, only to introduce a squeeze within a few months; they believed that the British people would vote against the 'Suez adventurers', the 'Hola Camp murderers'.

Gaitskell and his colleagues were encouraged by the poor showing which the government put up in the opinion polls, all of which, early in 1959, showed that in the event of an election the Labour Party would win an overwhelming victory. In a sense this was to be expected for an historical reason; the Tories had won the 1951 and 1955 elections. No government in modern times had ever won three elections. The Tories simply could not win.

Harold Macmillan

The Labour Party and the opinion pollsters reckoned without Macmillan. The Earl of Winton recalls: 'When he became Prime Minister in January, 1957 Harold Macmillan succeeded to a gloomy inheritance. At home the Conservative Party was split and shaken. Abroad, Great Britain had declined in stature and repute; the economic situation was rocky; and worst of all there had been a disastrous deterioration in Anglo-American relations'.

Macmillan appreciated the problems in front of him. He succeeded in keeping

55 Cummings, in *The Daily Express*, illustrates the bewilderment of the floating voter in the first TV-dominated election. While the Labour Party accused the Tories of being a party of fault and defects, the floating voter could see that the Labour Party's record and programme was itself a messy affair

"I thought your shirt was off-white —— until I saw yours!"

56 Hugh Gaitskell (on the left) the young leader of the Labour Party, with Herbert Morrison who had hoped to succeed Attlee when he retired in 1955

his Party together, uniting once again both the 'Suez adventurers' and the few who had opposed this war. He decided that his government would have to go in for economic expansion. His Chancellor, Thorneycroft, with his Treasury colleagues Enoch Powell and Nigel Birch, opposed this. Macmillan allowed them to resign and appointed Heathcott Amory to be Chancellor to preside over a dismantling of the credit squeeze. The Bank rate was brought down throughout 1958 and 1959; hire purchase restrictions were removed one after the other so that by mid-1959 people could buy cars, washing machines, TV sets and refrigerators without having to put down any deposit and were allowed to repay their debt over a long period. Banks were encouraged to give their customers long-term loans.

By mid-1959 the economic picture had completely changed. Macmillan told the House of Commons: 'Every Hon. Member knows that for the mass of the people there has never been such a good time or such a high standard of living. I repeat what I said at Bedford, they have "never had it so good".'

Foreign affairs

Macmillan inherited a difficult situation in 1957 with America taking up an anti-British line and world opinion hostile to the British warmongers. Macmillan put this right as Herbert Morrison recalled:

Throughout the early months of 1959 the Labour Party was pressing the government to advocate a 'summit conference' and for the Prime Minister to make the first move by visiting Moscow ... Macmillan's carefully-gauged increase of enthusiasm for the two projects was cleverly contrived, thereby adding to his reputation as a man of peace and a progressive Tory ... The visit of President Eisenhower to London took place with an election in the offing ... The culmination of the visit with both men appearing on British television,

83

offered wonderful election propaganda on the eve of the announcement of the polling date ... The occasion was exploited to the maximum to build up a picture of a man of high international standing.

The election

In September 1959 Macmillan asked the Queen to dissolve Parliament and to call a general election for 8 October. Macmillan merely asked the electorate to vote for the government which had produced a situation in which 'they had never had it so good'. The Tory posters read: 'Tory freedom works; don't let Labour ruin it'—a sensible appeal for a successful government to make. Outside bodies, such as Tate and Lyle, organised campaigns paid for out of company profits to show the British people that nationalisation was a disaster and that private enterprise (Tory freedom again) really worked best. In glossy magazines this message was dropped through millions of letter-boxes and was reinforced by advertisements in the press and on the hoardings.

The Labour Party campaign never really got under way; many of the leaders were uncertain what to say about nationalisation. Some wanted to advocate more; others thought that this issue would not win much support in the country. The result, as Morrison recalls, was 'a failure to deal adequately with the election campaign of vilification of nationalised industries'.

The Labour Party had hoped to win votes as the party of international law and fairness, accusing the Tories of being warmongers. However, they were disappointed. In the first place foreign affairs rarely count in a British election; people are much more influenced by home affairs—which, under Macmillan, meant a vote for the Tories. Secondly the Labour Party found that its anti-Suez, pro-United Nations stand did not gain the favourable opinion of the majority of people, who did not take much interest in foreign affairs. Morrison wrote: 'the electorate had gained the idea that the Labour Party was anti-British and pro other nations which contrived complaints. This was largely a fallacious belief of course, but understandable'.

Morrison might have done better to recall what he had said when Nasser first invaded the Canal. Speaking in the Commons, he had said: 'This pocket dictator in Cairo does not consult his Parliament ... There is no discussion with us or other parties to the Convention ... This action is morally wrong .. I refuse to speak a single syllable in justification of what Colonel Nasser has done

Result

Contrary to the opinion pollsters and against the run of history, Macmillan and his Tories won the third of the 1950s elections. Not only did they win but they increased their majority as they won 365 seats whilst the Labour Party won only 258. The miniscule Liberal Party with 6 seats fell even further from grace.

For Macmillan it was a great triumph and he seemed to deserve the nickname 'Supermac' which had first been given him in fun. For Gaitskell and the Labour

57 This cartoon from *The Observer*, 1958, shows that idealism was of little use to the Labour Party and Mr Gaitskell; the voters preferred the affluence offered by Mr Macmillan

Party the result was a disaster. The party split even further over the issues of socialism and nationalisation. Gaitskell and his right-wing friends argued that the Labour Party should drop these old-fashioned ideas, change its constitution which bound it to 'nationalise the means of production, distribution and exchange' and even argued that perhaps it should change its name from Labour—with the suggestion of cloth caps, mining valleys and unemployment queues, to something brighter and more 'with it'.

The wrangling in the Labour Party reached new heights of bitterness at Annual Conferences in 1960 and 1961 when left-wing members of the Party succeeded (in 1960) in getting it to accept the principle of British unilateral disarmament, only to be told by Gaitskell that he and others would 'fight, fight, and fight again to save the Party' from such madness. Would the Labour Party ever unite? Could it formulate policies which would please its various factions? Would it appeal to the people again? In 1960 there were many who doubted this and reporters began to write about the inevitability of permanent Tory rule.

58 'Trog', in *The Spectator*, showed Mr Macmillan with members of his 'Cabinet' on the morning after the 1959 election. The status symbols of the affluent society had convinced the electorate that Tory freedom worked

'Well, gentlemen, I think we all fought a good fight . . .'

Tory socialism

In the 1930s many countries in Europe became dominated by either Fascist or Communist Parties. In Portugal, Spain, Italy and Germany, Fascist-type parties of the right wing were in power; similar governments ruled in countries in the Balkans—Hungary, Romania, Albania, Greece and so on. Opposed to these was the Communist government of Russia with its very strong satellite parties in France and other countries.

Only in Britain was the right-left struggle not a feature of political life. Oswald Mosley tried to create a Fascist party in Britain, and failed; the Communist Party never had a membership of more than a couple of hundred thousand. One of the reasons for this lack of polarisation was the success of the Tory Party in becoming a party of the middle. It had once been a party of the landed aristocrat (Chapter 3) but under Disraeli it had become a party supported by many of the working class. Under Baldwin in the 1920s and 1930s the Tory Party was a party of the centre, of the middle ground. As Baldwin himself said: 'I am opposed to socialism but I have always tried to make the Conservative Party face left in its anti-socialism'. By this he meant that he had tried to get the Party to accept many of the socialists' ideas.

Post-war Toryism

When they lost the 1945 election the Tories did not 'retire to their tents' as Fox did after 1784 (Chapter 1). Churchill appointed Lord Woolton to become Party Chairman and, aided by Maxwell-Fyfe he carried out a major reorganisation of the Tory Party. In the Conservative Central Office, R. A. Butler headed a team including Ian MacLeod, Reginald Maudling, Enoch Powell and Quintin Hogg, who worked out a series of policies which the next Tory government should carry out.

When the Tories came back to office under Churchill and then under Eden many of these policies were put into practice. Indeed, some reporters thought that there was so little difference between the policies of Butler, the Tory, and Gaitskell, his Labour predecessor at the Treasury, that they coined the word 'Butskellism' to indicate the socialist policy being followed by the Tory governments.

Under Macmillan the process continued. He wrote:

It is very difficult for those whose memories do not go back to the twenties and thirties to have any conception of the virulence with which the role of the

59 Winston Churchill with his wife, after hearing that the Tories had won the 1951 election. 'Winnie's back' was one headline

State in a modern economy was contested . . . Any form of State intervention was believed to be necessarily incompetent, and the prelude to some form of dictatorship. Some of the most intelligent and responsible leaders in many fields of national life had supported *laissez-faire* on these grounds.

Nevertheless, much of what I was advocating in those years has come about: a National Economic Development Council; a government which controls the Central Bank, and assumes responsibility for the general level of economic activity through the Bank rate and the Budget; extensions of the public utility principle in transport and fuel; even some welfare distribution of essential

60 Vicky had intended to ridicule Macmillan by showing him as a Supermac, drawing the crowds. The series of cartoons only increased the electorate's admiration for the man who could reunite the Tory Party, restore Britain's friendship with America, organise a series of meetings with the Russians and head a government which raised living standards—Supermac indeed!

foods, such as the expanded schools meals service and the milk, orange-juice and cod-liver oil for mothers and babies. The era of strict *laissez-faire* has passed into history, together with the derelict towns, the boarded-up shops and the barefooted children, and—above all—the long rows of men and women outside the Labour Exchanges.

But the challenge to our intelligence remains, though the difficulties with which we must wrestle are almost precisely the reverse of those that beset us in the thirties. An overstrained economy with constant anxiety about the balance of payments, shortage of labour, and an inflation that has generated a new insecurity . . . these are the problems with which contemporary statesmen must concern themselves.

Taxation

But the cost of social progress is increased taxation; someone has to pay for the hospitals, schools, welfare clinics and so on; for the pensions and other benefits given by the State; and the ever-increasing wages bill required by teachers, nurses, doctors and civil servants. In the 1930s Chamberlain had apologised when, owing to rearmament, the standard rate of tax was raised to 5s [25p] in the £. Since 1945 we have become accustomed to a standard rate around the 35p to 40p mark, while those with incomes of above £5,000 a year also have to contend with super-tax which, at its highest, rises to around 90p in the £. In addition to this high level of direct taxation—the highest in Europe—there are the countless indirect taxes on petrol, cigarettes and most of the goods bought over the counters of the nation's shops.

Expenditure

This government revenue is spent in various ways—on defence, on aid to industry, as well as on social welfare. Whereas all classes can be seen to gain from the nation's defence as well as from government aid to industry, it is the less well-off who benefit most obviously from such payments as National Assistance,

61 The motorcar, symbol of affluence. The number of cars continues to increase

62 London dockers marching to the House of Commons in support of Enoch Powell, who was opposed to Labour's Race Relations Bill, 1968

Family Allowances and so on. By 1959, the high spot of the Macmillan era, this country had become 'the affluent society' in comparison with the state of affairs in the 1930s or the 1940s. Many of the old middle classes—or professional people—resented the rising standard of living being enjoyed by the formerly less well-off. Letters to newspapers, answers to interviewers on radio and television programmes indicated a generally widely held idea that 'there are hundreds of Jaguars clogging up the streets on council house estates, where the highly-paid worker is living in a cheap house for which the middle-class taxpayer is paying a subsidy'.

In 1953, Sir Philip Gibbs, a journalist, wrote:

The Welfare State has to be paid for. It is supported by income tax, surtax and death duties which annihilate the ancient prerogatives of wealth.

The so-called working classes have received a good many benefits and have the illusion of a new prosperity. The benefits are real enough. The old grinding poverty has gone for all who have a job and a wage. One no longer sees people in rags. No longer does one see skinny, white-faced children in tattered frocks and bare feet. The awful dread of the poor-house no longer haunts the minds of labourers and their wives and children. I remember all that in my boyhood, and shudder at the thought of it.

I for one rejoice in the new prosperity of the great mass of people in this country. But an illusion is there, alas. Some of this new money is like fairy gold. How long is the fairy tale going to last—how long the real benefits to the former poor who are now the new rich?

But one thing is fairly certain; the prospect of a continuance of high taxation and low-level living. For, if we are quite honest about it, this beautiful vision of a Welfare State does not provide beyond the necessities of life for a large number of people in this crowded island.

Toughness and power

Why did Tory governments continue to follow a semi-socialist policy if their main supporters—the middle class—resented it? Disraeli had been the first

Tory to point out that in a democratic society power would lie with the party which could win the largest share of the working-class vote.

Failure to carry out policies appealing to the working class could only result in the Tory Party becoming less popular, as Mr Macmillan found in 1962–1963:

> The government's electoral battering early in 1962 gave rise to rumours that Mr Macmillan intended to reshuffle his Cabinet. On 12 July at Leicester North-West the Conservative candidate finished an ignominious third, 10 per cent behind the Liberal. The next day the Chancellor of the Exchequer was sacked along with the Lord Chancellor and five other Cabinet Ministers. Many believed Macmillan was 'mainly acting in desperation because of the government's recent by-election defeats'.

> Meanwhile Britain was enduring its worst winter since 1881. The economy had been sick throughout 1962. Now bad weather led to mounting unemployment. The number of unemployed rose to 2.5 per cent of the labour force in December 1962 (compared with 1.7 per cent a year earlier); in February 1963 the total reached 3.9 per cent, the highest figure since the fuel crisis of 1947. The number who feared unemployment was even higher; in December, 19 per cent of a Gallup sample [opinion poll] believed that they, or a member of their family, would be affected. The regions farthest from London were particularly hard hit; in February, 7 per cent of the labour force were out of work in the North-East, 6 per cent in Scotland and 6 per cent in Wales. During the late winter Conservative murmurings against Mr Macmillan's leadership could be heard.

Labour governments, 1964–1970

This unpopularity died down in 1964 as the Tory Chancellor, Reginald Maudling, created an economic boom—on the pattern laid down by Mr Butler and Mr Amory in 1955 and 1959 respectively (Chapter 9). However, the Tory recovery came too late in 1964 and the Wilson government took office with an overall majority of only 3. In March 1966 Wilson called another general election and increased his majority. To many people it seemed that Mr Wilson was as 'super' as Macmillan had been in 1959; many reporters suggested that perhaps we were entering on a period of permanent Labour rule since its policies and ideas were more in line with the demands of the rising working class, who liked the Wilson idea that 'In Cabinet and boardroom alike, those with responsibility must be able to speak with the language of the technical age. For the commanding heights of industry to be controlled by men whose only claim is aristocratic connection, or the power of wealth, is as irrelevant to the twentieth century as would be the continued purchase of commissions in the armed forces by lordly amateurs. At the very time when the MCC has abandoned the distinction between amateur and professional, we are content to remain, in science and industry, a nation of gentlemen in a world of players'.

63 Edward Heath making his final tour of his constituency of Bexleyheath, Kent, during the 1970 election campaign

But by 1970 the Labour government's popularity had fallen as sharply as had that of Mr Macmillan's government. An almost continuous credit squeeze, a high level of unemployment, the abandonment of the socialist idea of a free Health Service, the devaluation of the pound—all these had made this government seem one of the least efficient the country had had since the war.

Even worse, it appeared also to be one of the most cowardly; having decided that trade union reform was needed and having produced a White Paper outlining the reforms considered necessary, the government backed down faced with trade union opposition and did not press on with its promised Industrial Relations Bill.

Election 1970
However, as the run up to the general election got under way, the government managed to recover some at least of its popularity with the trade unions—after the dropping of the Industrial Relations Bill. The credit squeeze and the wages freeze were ended. Wage increases of 15 per cent, 20 per cent and even 30 per cent were negotiated as one after another the trade unions won concessions from their employers. The housewife saw the effects of this in ever-rising prices of goods in the shops; the government hoped that contentment with rising wages would be greater than the discontent with rising prices.

The opinion polls seemed to show that the government had judged the nation's mood correctly. It was a very quiet election campaign in which there was little mention of serious issues but a good deal of personal abuse was thrown at and by the Party leaders. Mr Wilson and the Labour Party were comforted by the opinion polls which showed that they would win the third election in succession, so emulating Macmillan and the Tories in the 1950s.

The result
Few people shared the optimism of the Tory leader, Edward Heath, who asked people to look at the continuing rise in prices. He promised that if the Tories were returned they would reduce 'at a stroke' the level of price increases. Many people believed that he was promising to bring down prices—which is another matter.

The first few results shown on the nation's TV screens showed that the Labour

Party and the opinion polls had misjudged things very badly. When all the results were in, the Tories had won 330 seats to Labour's 287 and the Liberal's 6. After six years of Labour rule the country had decisively turned to the Tories again.

The effects

But within a year, opinion polls were again recording massive swings in public opinion to the Labour Party, while several by-elections held in this year showed that this time, at any rate, the polls were telling the truth. The Labour Party won a seat from the Tories at Bromsgrove, while even 'safe' Tory seats with majorities of over 10,000 seemed to be in danger, as was shown at Maccles-field in October 1971, where a majority of 11,000 at the general election slumped to a majority of only 1,100 at the by-election.

Why this sudden change in popularity? Mr Heath's government kept many of the promises it had made at the election. One of its first moves was to cut taxation, which should have been popular. But a cut in taxation had to be met by a cut in government expenditure. The Heath government decided that in future people would pay a higher proportion of the cost of dental and medical treatment—so saving money for the government and allowing taxes to be cut. But the taxpayer who was also paying more to the dentist, optician or chemist, found that he was no better off, unless he was a very rich taxpayer getting a large rebate from the government. As for the millions who do not pay income tax, they stood only to lose since they had to pay the increased charges and received none of the benefits of the tax cuts.

Another way in which the government saved money was by cutting back on the assistance previously paid to various industries. In future, said John Davies, the new Minister of Trade and Technology, there would be less aid for 'lame ducks'. When he used that phrase at the Conservative Party Conference in 1970, just after the election, he received a thunder of applause. By the winter of 1971–1972 this 'lame duck' policy had led to the bankruptcy of, among others, the Upper Clyde Shipbuilders, Rolls Royce, two aircraft firms and a host of smaller companies. Taxpayers may have been relieved to know that their money wasn't going to be 'handed out' to these firms. The ever-increasing number of unemployed were less happy; in particular the highly-skilled and the managerial executives were bewildered by their fate. Most of these had voted Tory and found that the new Toryism meant redundancy.

New Toryism

The essence of the new Toryism is that the government should only do for people what they cannot do for themselves. The really poor, the sick and disabled, the unemployed and unemployable will be helped; but for the rest, there is a market price which has to be paid for goods and services and the government will not interfere to lessen that price. Both the abolition of free school milk for children under the age of 11, the increases in council house rents by, on average, 50 per

64 John Davies, Minister of Trade and Industry, and the author of the 'lame duck' speech, in which he said that the Conservative government would not subsidise loss-making industries

cent will save the taxpayers money but will mean an increased expenditure by the children's parents, or by council house tenants.

This is a different Toryism from that practised by Baldwin, Butler, Eden and Macmillan. This is a Toryism in which success will be rewarded and failure punished.

Author's note

The body of the text was written early in 1972, as the use of the present tense in the final paragraph indicates. In the year that has passed since then the Heath government has had a number of changes of heart—and of policies. Newspaper headlines have called these changes 'U-turns'. A disgruntled Conservative MP has declared 'The government has stood on its head so often that there are now no more heads left to stand on'. Mr Heath has begun to realise that a modern, industrialised society cannot be run on free-swinging, private-enterprise lines. He has been forced to undo much of what he has done and to do things that he announced he would not do. In 1973 he has used the slogan 'Fair shares for all'—which is a far cry from the headier days of 1970.

Further Reading

Documentary collections which include material on elections:
T. Charles-Edwards and B. Richardson, *They Saw It Happen* 1689–1897 (Blackwell)
Asa Briggs, *They Saw It Happen* 1897–1940 (Blackwell)
G. A. Sambrook, *English Life in the Nineteenth Century* (Macmillan)
D. Holman, *Portraits and Documents; earlier 19th century* 1783–1867 (Hutchinson)

Autobiographies of leading politicians provide interesting material. Among these are:
Herbert Morrison, *An Autobiography* (Odhams)
Lord Samuel, *Memoirs* (London, 1945)
Viscount Snowden, *Memoirs* (Cresset Press)
Hugh Dalton, *High Tide and After* and other volumes (Muller)
Earl of Avon (Anthony Eden), *Full Circle* and other volumes (Cassell)
Harold Macmillan, *Wind of Change* and other volumes (Macmillan)
Clement Attlee, *A Prime Minister Remembers* (Heinemann)
(Relatives or family friends might very well have their own memories of past elections)

General Works which can be used to provide economic and social background include:
Asa Briggs, *The Age of Improvement* 1783–1867 (Longman)
G. D. H. Cole and R. W. Postgate, *The Common People* (Methuen)
Pauline Gregg, *A Social and Economic History of Britain Since* 1776 (Harrap)
A. F. Havighurst, *Twentieth Century Britain* (Harper and Row)
C. L. Mowat, *Britain Between the Wars* 1919–1940 (Methuen)
H. Nicholson, *King George V: his life and reign* (Constable)
Robert Kee, *The Day before Yesterday* (Sidgwick and Jackson)
Peter Lane, *A History of Post-war Britain* (Macdonald)

Periods and personalities. Books dealing with specific shorter periods:
G. M. Trevelyan, *Grey of the Reform Bill* (Longman)
Philip Magnus, *Gladstone* (John Murray)
Robert Blake, *Disraeli* (Eyre and Spottiswoode)
Roy Jenkins, *Balfour's Poodle* (Heinemann)
J. B. Priestley, *The Edwardians* (Heinemann)
R. R. James, *Lord Randolph Churchill* (Weidenfeld and Nicolson)
W. Rodgers and B. Donoghue, *The People into Parliament*

Jackdaws (Jonathan Cape) No 16: The Vote 1832–1928; No 49: Women in Revolt—the fight for emancipation

Then and There Series (Longman): *Parliamentary Elections and Reform; The Chartists; Edwardian England; Suffragettes and Votes for Women; Keir Hardie and the Labour Party*

Index

Numbers in *Italic type* refer to the pages on which illustrations appear.

PRINCIPAL.
REGIONAL TECHNICAL COLLEGE,
PORT ROAD,
LETTERKENNY.